*For Bryant: Warmest
your burgeoning jour*

Byliners

Cedric

23/4/18

101 ways to be a freelance journalist

*Bylines, our name on an article, are our credentials as
writing freelances. They spell confidence not only in editors
but also in sources we wish to interview. Top byliners are
so valuable to a newspaper that they are able to make
special deals*

www.pulfordmedia.co.uk/ituri

Also from Cedric Pulford and Ituri

JournoLISTS: 201 Ways to Improve Your Journalism

Air Madness: Road's Mistakes Repeated (environment)

Casualty of Empire (history)

Eating Uganda (history/religion)

Our Vanishing Freedoms (politics) pamphlet

Siren Society (politics)

About the author

Cedric Pulford has had a 40-year career in journalism, much of it as a freelance. He enjoyed a long association with the Guardian/Observer newspaper group, and was a foreign correspondent based in London for news media in Switzerland and Canada. He is now a busy writer with six books to his credit.

Rick is also one of Britain's most experienced training consultants, running a Successful Freelancing course. He has degrees in political subjects from Oxford and Case Western Reserve universities, and lives in rural Northamptonshire.

Byliners

101 ways to be a freelance journalist

Cedric Pulford

ITURI

Byliners published 2009 by Ituri Publications
4 Chestnut Close
Woodford Halse
Northants NN11 3NB (UK)
ISBN **9780953643097**

Text set in 11pt on 14pt Palatino
with headings in Arial
by Book Production Services, London

Printed and bound in the UK by 4edge Limited
www.4edge.co.uk

FSC Mixed Sources
SA-COC-001695
FSC © 1996 FSC A.C.

*This book uses environmentally friendly papers certified by the Forest
Stewardship Council*

Contents

INTRODUCTION/ ACKNOWLEDGEMENTS

The 101 tips presented in this book have a mixed ancestry. Taken together, much has come from my 30-year career as a newspaper freelance. I was variously the UK correspondent for a business newsletter in Canada and a Geneva-based religious news agency, a contributor to British national newspapers and a writer/editor for the Guardian's syndication service.

But no individual freelance can see the whole battlefield. I have to thank the many contributors to the Freelance Forum in the British Association of Journalists' newsletter. I edited this column for a decade, and the experiences which the contributors generously shared have greatly enlarged my knowledge of the field. In particular, my fellow BAJ member, Judy Yorke, has supplied two valuable insights (p95 and p113).

My horizon has been enlarged by the Successful Freelancing course which I ran in association with the National Council for the Training of Journalists. Attendees brought reports from the front line, keeping us all up to speed.

The sequence of the chapters, and the content of the book overall, closely follow those of the Successful Freelancing course. In that sense, **Byliners** is a course between book covers. It's a "rock face" book of down-to-earth suggestions. I hope it proves interesting and of value to freelances at every level of experience, from the beginner to the veteran.

Thanks are due to my Pulford Media colleague, Roderick Thomson, who proof-read the **Byliners** manuscript and made numerous helpful comments. Needless to say, any mistakes are entirely mine. I'd be happy to hear from any reader with comments or corrections, using the contact details on the title verso (the back of the title page).

It would have been easy to write a longer book than this one. I decided that brevity would serve the subject better. Each of the 101 tips is never less than 200 words and never more than 400 words. The average length is 300 words. This formalisation is intended to help the practical usefulness of **Byliners**. Sometimes it involved discreet bumping out to length. More often, it meant cutting back over-luxuriant growth. Cutting and expanding are key journalistic skills. I hope you can't see the joins.

1 OPPORTUNITIES

Freelance journalism is the ultimate open market. Refreshingly in this age of registrations, accreditations and qualifications, freelance journalism remains what it has always been: an open market, aka a free-for-all. You are a freelance journalist if you say you are. Of course, if you never have any material published it's an empty title. But it does mean we can be off and running without fuss, bother or a vast upfront investment. Start with optimism and confidence, and the bylines (our name on an article, usually at the top) will follow.

Qualifications – whether general educational ones like degrees or specifics like knowledge of a particular subject – may mean we produce better material. We shall probably be asked to register to attend a conference as a journalist. We are accredited when we are issued with a press card by one of several issuing organisations (although, importantly, never by the government). But all of these things are optional extras. We don't need them to ply our trade.

Some freelance journalists make fortunes. These are almost always in areas where not everyone wants to go: celebrity trivia, royal exclusives and muck-raking exposes. For most freelances it's hard graft for an adequate but not sensational return.

The British Association of Journalists – one of the three main trade unions for journalists – in a survey of print media freelances found that they made on average around four-fifths of the earnings of full-time staff journalists. More than half of the freelances worked at least 40 hours a week. Yet just one respondent among the 22 in this survey would trade in the life for a staff job. Freelances gain in so many other ways than money – being your own boss, no more tedious commutes to the office, flexibility about when you work, for example.

Freelancing can be full-time, part-time or between staff jobs. The flexibility of freelance journalism is one of its most appealing aspects. The field is ideal for working part-time or as a supplement to the income from your day job. The editor with whom you deal won't know – and won't care – whether you are a full-time or part-time freelance.

Many people are happy to stay as part-timers, perhaps because the activity is an add-on to another job. Or they are trying out freelancing to see if it's the life for them. Between staff jobs, they may want to see if they can make a go of it and stay as self-employed.

For the first-time freelance, working part-time before going full-time makes sense. Among the issues to be considered are loneliness and distraction, as well as a fluctuating, non-guaranteed income.

Not everyone can cope with long hours working in isolation, with only the phone and the internet for company. We get through a lot of work that way – if we don't lose edge without the stimulus of being with other people. Some freelances prefer not to work from home but share offices with other freelances.

The home is a distracting place, particularly with young children around. Journalism needs concentration, and it's usually fatal to try to combine child-minding with researching and writing an article. However, having an inviolable time and space for work is more easily said than done for many people.

Another form of distraction is where we do anything to put off getting down to the article. As Barbara Ellen put it in the *Observer*: "Lurking aimlessly by the kettle is a perennial favourite. Snoozing a must – I call them powerless naps. Then there's important stuff like counting your freckles."

Just like full-timers, part-time freelances need to be ready to respond to rush jobs. So they aren't entirely the master of their timetable. When an editor calls, it's no answer to say that today isn't our day for working. That's a good way of losing work for keeps.

Competition is fierce; we need a niche. The corollary of freelance journalism as a free market (see above) is that there are a lot of people at it. They include retired staff journalists, who may be formidable competitors. It means that we need to identify and develop a niche for ourselves.

A niche is a specialist area that we are well suited to write about. We should begin by asking ourselves which are the areas where we have special knowledge or interest. If we have both, so much the better. We need to be able to match and hopefully surpass others working in this area.

Knowledge or interest isn't enough, however. There has to be a market for our work. This is partly a matter of how interesting the media are in the subject; it's also how crowded the field is with other freelances.

Health is an area for which there is an apparently insatiable demand, with the inevitable glut of writers. We may have to settle for less obvious subjects like archaeology or urban planning, which are nevertheless able to generate interesting material.

Some areas are full of cronies of the editors who commission the articles. Travel and motoring, which generate attractive freebies, are cases in point.

Another sort of niche is the newspaper or magazine we write for. In general, it's better to build a position with one publication rather than spread our work among many. This is a bit of a balancing act because, on the other hand, we don't want all our eggs in one basket. The question is explored later in the book.

An important aim – which will be in the future for beginning freelances – is for editors to come to us to commission an article (see Chapter 5) rather than us always going to them with ideas. Editors won't approach us unless (a) they know us and (b) like our work.

A 'bread and butter' activity complements freelancing. Earnings from freelancing are by their nature fluctuating; food and utility bills aren't. It's helpful to have a steady source of income to look after many of the necessities.

Of course, for a part-timer the day job is that staple. For the full-time freelance who wants a "bread and butter" sideline, the possibilities include casual shifts on newspapers and magazines, teaching, writing press releases for small businesses and proof-reading.

A major advantage of the *casual shift* is that it's "hermetically sealed" from the rest of our work. We can forget about it all week long except when we go in for our shift (when naturally we give it 100%).

Shifts have always been easier to find in sub-editing than in reporting. Paradoxically, the best way for the writing freelance to succeed as a shift-worker is to learn sub-editing! That is, not only the computer programs but also the journalism techniques like headline writing, caption writing, cutting and condensing. Short courses are readily available in both aspects of the craft.

Getting that first tryout can be hard, but provided our application is halfway credible most publications will give us a go for a day or two.

National newspapers have a big appetite for casuals, but the system reaches far beyond that. It's worth asking about opportunities on local newspapers and quite small magazines. The increasing maternity and paternity benefits for staff workers can only increase the prospects for casuals to fill the gaps.

Recent years have seen an explosion of media studies at various levels. Students are keen to hear from "real journalists" – not media sociologists – so with some experience under our belt we become an attractive proposition to hire as *part-time lecturers*.

Small and medium-sized businesses all over the country are missing out on promotional opportunities because they have no press office and no-one who knows how to write an acceptable press release. We can help these businesses by acting as their *press release writers*.

Against a general decline in the standards of written English, these enterprises can also benefit from *proof-readers* who check both copy and typeset material. So much proof-reading in newspapers, magazines and books is done in-house (or not done) that proof-reading opportunities in the wider world are, regretfully, limited.

Features are easier to place than news. National newspapers have the entire United Kingdom covered with a network of freelance correspondents. So does the Press Association – PA – the famous national news agency, which was a co-operative owned by the nation's press and which has since been privatised.

The correspondents file news stories from their areas, or may be called upon to cover a story the paper has heard about. These correspondents, or *stringers*, may be journalists on local newspapers, who supplement their meagre wages by recycling their stories for the national press, or they may work in locally based news agencies. (These sometimes poach stories from the staff journalists who wrote them!)

The same pattern of stringers is repeated with regional dailies, many of which, like the *Yorkshire Post* or the *Western*

Morning News (Plymouth), cover huge areas.

All of this makes news an extremely unpromising area for the incoming freelance, unless he or she tries to hook up with a news agency, which may or may not have a vacancy at that time. Certainly, we can place news stories with small newspapers or with trade and technical magazines. However, pay rates are so small as to make the exercise hardly worthwhile (except as a source of cuttings with which we can leverage more remunerative work).

With features, the position is entirely different. Features are founded on ideas (news is founded on events), and no-one has a monopoly of ideas. Therefore publications will look at proposals for features from wherever they come.

Features in newspapers have the advantage of being a growing market. Papers have expanded, and grown sections. Much of the extra editorial space is filled by features. Editors know that it's cheaper to fill space with features rather than news, but they have also reminded themselves of the newspaper pioneer Lord Northcliffe's dictum: "Hard news catches readers, features hold them." No-one knows this better, and acts upon it, than the *Daily Mail*, the newspaper Lord Northcliffe founded.

Websites and email news services are good ways to get started. Few beginning freelances are fortunate enough to start at the top, with national newspapers and national consumer magazines. The rest have to start somewhere else, and professional websites and email news services are a good way of building up confidence and a portfolio. The journalism techniques of researching and gathering information are the same; so is the writing even if material on websites is a little shorter.

We aren't talking about a publication that appears concurrently on paper and online, but sites and services that exist only on the internet. These seem bound to increase in the years ahead.

The explosion of blogs, some of which are good but many of which are amateurish, means that being published on the web doesn't by itself bring us any professional credit. It all depends who we write for. Traditionally, writing for the internet hasn't enjoyed the same professional standing as writing for print. This is reflected in lower fees.

This distinction between net and print is becoming harder to maintain. While the jury remains out on whether print publications will ever disappear, ever more readers are willing to take their information via the net. For example, for academics – who were early adopters of search engines – taking learned journals online has become commonplace.

Publishers are looking to a future beyond print. We'd do well to go with them.

Don't ignore the trade and technical press. As the name indicates, the trade and technical press comprises specialist publications for particular occupations or interests. *Farmers Weekly*, *Pulse* (for doctors), *Fairplay* (for the shipping industry) and *Horse and Hound* (made famous in the film, *Notting Hill)* are among hundreds in the UK alone. Many are important forces in their communities, although not widely known to the general public. We should be proud to work for them.

Trade and technical publications pay less well than consumer magazines like *Homes and Gardens* or *Woman's Own*. But competition to place material is less and the sub-editors are likely to be less finicky – a characteristic of the top-end glossy mags. A regular connection can build up into a steady source of income. This is more useful than infrequent, higher-paying one-offs.

The huge number of these magazines makes them ideal for the freelance who has, wisely, resolved to specialise. This in turn can lead to commissions from national newspapers. If you were a commissioning editor on the *Daily Telegraph*, who would be more likely to sell you on the idea of a feature about trains – a contributor to *Railway Magazine* or a jobbing freelance with nothing to show in that area?

Small businesses need our public relations expertise. Marketing, or rather the lack of it, is said to be the greatest weakness of small businesses. Firms need a substantial scale before they can afford to employ a PR person. Smaller operations, even though their turnover may be several million pounds, are too busy running the show to pay much attention to promotion. Somebody may be designated to handle press inquiries, but chances are that he or she will fit it in grudgingly with the day job, and not do it very well.

Here is an excellent opportunity for the freelance who wants to develop a staple activity as suggested above. The most immediate need is for decently written press releases when the firm has something to announce. Another useful service is proof-reading. This is a euphemism for knocking poorly written, confusing or ambiguous raw material into shape for anything from intranet items to the company's annual report. Detailed knowledge of the particular company's operations isn't needed: the application of basic journalism skills will make us seem like miracle workers!

The difficulty is how to let firms know about our services. Most immediately practicable is to focus on small firms across a range of activities in the area where we live. We can create our target list from Yellow Pages, local "shopper" magazines or other reference sources. A mailshot (probably still better than email), *followed by a phone call a couple of weeks later*, is the likeliest way to get a result. We might give a before-and-after example to show how an effective press release can be created from messy raw material.

When we phone, we ask to speak to whoever deals with press inquiries. We may get blocked at this stage but, provided we sound confident, we'll probably be put through to somebody whether this is the owner, the chief executive or the poor soul who really does deal with press inquiries. They may say they never saw the mailshot. But at least we have their ear – and we start again with a spoken pitch.

Sounds like hard work? It is. Not what you're in journalism for? It isn't. But it gets results.

Opportunities abound abroad if you know where to look. The importance of the UK means that nations around the world are keen for news and views from here. The best prospects are with foreign magazines. Major newspapers have syndication agreements with their British counterparts, and are unlikely to want additional material.

We don't need to confine ourselves to the English-speaking world. Many other countries are used to receiving articles in English and translating them. The names and contact details of major foreign newspapers and magazines appear in directories like Benn's and Willings, to be found in main public libraries.

The usual approach is to send an email asking whether the publication would be interested to look at an article on such-and-such. We must hope that foreign editors have better manners than their UK counterparts, who usually ignore such messages (see below), but we shouldn't be surprised if we get no reply.

It's better not to send an unsolicited article, but if we haven't made contact this becomes our best bet (*for foreign submissions, not home ones*). The coming of Skype and other VOIP (voice over internet protocol) channels means that phoning abroad is no longer prohibitively expensive. However, complications of time zones, locating the person we wish to talk with and possible language issues mean that phone calls remain an impracticable option.

Writing for foreign publications has the added attraction that the same piece can be sold in several markets at the same time. We can do that where there is no overlap in readerships – between Australia and the Netherlands, for example.

A freelance journalist who tries to crack foreign markets should be prepared to find it harder work than doing so at home. Sometimes it seems as if we're sending material into a bottomless pit, never to be seen or heard from again. But the opportunities are enormous. We can boost ourselves with the thought that because they don't say yes, it doesn't mean they won't want the article when they see it!

2 QUALIFICATIONS

Journalism isn't a closed shop, but being in a trade union may help. Despite what many people think, journalism isn't and never has been a closed shop. That means you don't have to be in a trade union to work as a journalist, either full time or part-time

It was once common for almost every newspaper journalist to belong to the main union, the National Union of Journalists. The end of collective bargaining in most offices and the emergence of personal contracts made many staffers question the need to join a union. Membership has slumped – even more so in magazines than in newspapers.

It's against this background that an editor is very unlikely to ask you as a freelance whether you belong to a union. He or she won't care. Joining a union may be an excellent idea, however. This is principally for the range of legal and other advice that they provide. Copyright advice, contract issues and recommended fees are examples of ways a union can help. News of the industry also helps an isolated freelance to keep in touch.

In print journalism, there are three trade unions vying with each other for our support. The honour of being the oldest belongs to the Chartered Institute of Journalists, while the biggest and best known is the National Union of Journalists.

The British Association of Journalists is a relative newcomer, founded in the 1990s.

Before applying for membership, you should research the different character of these unions. The NUJ, for example, is more political than the others, which may turn you on or turn you off. Beginning freelances need to ask about eligibility criteria, which may require some percentage of income to derive from journalism. Keen as they are for recruits, unions don't hand out membership cards willy-nilly. Too many people pretend to be journalists as a cover for dodgy activities.

You don't need to be in a trade union to get a press card. As a member of a union, you will be issued with a card identifying you as a journalist. You won't be asked to show it very often to prove your *bona fides*. Some journalists find its greatest use is to blag free entry to shows and events in the guise of doing a story! This dishonest, although regrettably widespread, practice devalues journalism. It's one of the reasons why journalists rank with estate agents (and MPs!) at the bottom in public esteem. That said, there are obviously occasions when showing a press card is useful. Sometimes it helps when doing impromptu interviews with members of the public, for example.

Another type of card is more potent. This used to be called a "police press card", and is supposed to be issued only to road-going reporters (including freelances). It was so called because the card was, and is, recognised by the police, and may give the holder access denied to the public.

But you don't have to be in a union to obtain this card. They are issued both by unions and by proprietor organisations including the Newspaper Publishers Association, the Newspaper Society and the Periodical Publishers Association. Some 17 media organisations form a "gatekeepers' committee", which is responsible for the scheme.

A police press card is a useful form of identity in situations where security is tight – sure to increase in times to come. In 10 years of covering church affairs, one of the few occasions when I used this card was to enter Canterbury Cathedral in 2003 for the enthronement of Rowan Williams as Archbishop of Canterbury.

Your prior experience in life is your greatest qualification. A successful freelance journalist doesn't need to be a university graduate. With BAs more and more widespread, it may be hard to become a trainee journalist without a degree. But for you as a freelance, no-one will care a rap about your academic background. And once you've established yourself, the lack of a degree won't damage your chances of crossing over to staff journalism if that's what you want.

Of course, a degree may inform and improve your work as a journalist, although legions of non-graduates testify that it's far from essential. In four decades of journalism, I've never been asked by colleagues whether I'm a graduate. Nor have I known about their status except insofar as it comes out in casual conversation.

When asked what degree subject is best for journalism, many editors will say "Any". That's a bit of a cop-out. There would be wide agreement that English isn't the best subject. This is because the English studied at university has little to do with technical competence in functional English, as required for journalism. Craftsmen are needed, not litterateurs.

The most relevant degree subjects, many will say, are politics, economics and history. The first two have obvious connections to the stuff of news, while a sense of history (often weak with journalists) is vital for backgrounding a story.

But your life's experiences aren't only academic. Perhaps you have worked widely with people or know about the Majority World (aka the Third World) at first hand; perhaps you are good with numbers, a green activist, a political policy wonk, mad about computers, and so on. What you are, and what you've been, are what you bring to the table of journalism. So when choosing a specialism, it makes sense to play to your strengths.

Technical qualifications boost writing prospects. If you are writing about engineering, clearly being a member of the Institution of Mechanical Engineers will be a help. Medical doctors have an obvious advantage in writing about medicine and, in fact, many are drawn to be part-time journalists.

They find a ready market with editors, who know the value of the word "Dr" in the byline of a medical article. Same applies to us all. We shouldn't be bashful about putting to work any technical qualifications we may have.

The hazard of technically qualified people writing about their own area is that they fall into jargon or impenetrable detail. We have to remember that we are journalists first and technicians second!

Some people become freelance journalists to get away from their day job so this tip may seem unhelpful! Look on it then as providing a bread and butter staple, as described in Chapter 1. Putting our qualifications to work need not stop us building up a second specialism in a subject we enjoy. It's reasonable to have two specialisms, although having more than two risks spreading ourselves too thinly or – just as bad – confusing editors about what we specialise in.

The interpreter is more valuable than the opinioniser. Personal opinion pieces are the least promising form of freelancing. Editors have their arrangements in place. When a vacancy arises for a columnist, it's invariably filled by a staff journalist or a regular contributor – or a household name (whose article is probably ghosted).

Why should an editor offer this spot to an unknown contributor? Opinion writers, in fact, are 10 a penny; those who can produce a well sourced and interesting feature article on a topical issue are much more valuable.

Take the long-standing issue of Caesarean sections versus natural births. The World Health Organisation has deplored the rising trend of Caesareans in Western countries, much of it driven by social factors rather than medical need – the "too posh to push" brigade, doctors practising defensive medicine, and so on.

A news feature pegged to some new development around this issue – perhaps the latest statistics, or a senior figure criticising the WHO's stance, or a claim that obstetricians are performing Caesareans too willingly – will be more marketable than your opinion on the subject, or mine.

Such a feature, if it's to succeed, should be more than an assemblage of who said what and what happened. That is the province of the news story. The feature also needs to suggest what it *means* – in other words, to interpret the material. It does this, for example, by the use of background information, which puts the present situation into context, and by well chosen interpretative adjectives.

The difference between interpretation and opinion can be slippery, but it's highlighted by the comparison of "a *growing* preference for Caesarean sections" (interpretation, drawn from the facts) and "a *deplorable* preference for Caesarean sections" (our opinion – others will disagree).

Interpretation is a valuable skill for freelances while opinion is best left to the blogs.

If you don't write and spell well, learn to. The freelance who produces clean copy starts several furlongs down the track ahead of competitors. It gives editors confidence at a time when there are ever-fewer sub-editors to "fix it up".

The most important part of clean copy is the use of English at the functional level – that is, free of grammatical howlers and basic misspellings. The problem is that for many years grammar, spelling and punctuation has been an academic pariah subject. The mantra has been "It's what you feel about the subject that matters, not the mechanics of how you say it".

This has never been the view among journalists, any more than surgeons operate on the basis of how they feel about the human body rather than what they know about it. Clear and impactful English, including effective grammar, spelling and punctuation, is as essential to journalism as the scalpel is to the surgeon.

If you need to get your act together, there are any number of books to help. They include Lynne Truss's famous punctuation guide, *Eats, Shoots and Leaves* (2003). The classic *Waterhouse on Newspaper Style* (updated edition 1989) remains worth studying, not least because Keith Waterhouse has the credibility of someone who effectively practises what he preaches.

Journalism textbooks, including my own *JournoLISTS: 201 Ways to Improve Your Journalism* (2001), have examples of common grammar and spelling mistakes. Among the commonest is the misplaced apostrophe: *childrens' toys* and *womens' clothes* (should be *children's* and *women's*). *Between you and I* (*me*), *every dog has it's* (*its*) *day* and *the best* (*better*) *of the two* are common grammatical no-nos.

Embarass, harrass, accomodation, supercede, homogenous, a driving *license,* a *disinterested* student, the *principle* part, a rally *marshall* are all old friends we meet often – and every one is spelt wrongly. (But *license* is correct in the USA.)

Spellcheckers catch many of these mistakes, but they can't pick out a correctly spelt word in the wrong context: *complements to the chef,* for instance.

Watch out for guff like *adverse weather conditions* (*bad weather*) and *in spite of the fact that* (*although*) and long words where shorter words or phrases can be found: to *implement* is the same as to *carry out*; to *initiate* is the same as to *start*.

The freelance who avoids these mistakes has made an investment in success.

Shorthand is nice; a reliable audio recorder is nicer. The UK newspaper industry is obsessed with shorthand, which remains part of the qualifying exam for reporters, and easy-going about typing, which isn't tested. Yet Britain is in a minority among advanced countries in requiring shorthand. Typing is arguably the more important skill until the time when keyboards are superseded by voice inputting.

The case against compulsory shorthand lies in the numbers. The National Council for the Training of Journalists (NCTJ) sets a qualifying speed of 100 words per minute for newspaper reporters. When I ran Mirror Newspapers' editorial training scheme we had 120 wpm. Yet even this higher figure is well short of the speed at which people talk. TV newsreaders deliver at 180 wpm without seeming to rush, and the rest of us aren't far behind.

It follows that with 100 wpm shorthand, or even 120 wpm, the practical possibility of taking an accurate shorthand note is limited to two or three sentences – a small return for so much learning effort.

An even lower benchmark is set in the NCTJ's magazine journalism qualification – just 80 wpm. This is quite unrealistic in the real world. An undertaker would be prosecuted for speaking that slowly!

Shorthand is a useful skill, but it shouldn't be made into a sacred cow. Anyone who wants to learn shorthand should do so. But the rest of us can happily rely on an audio recorder and a good memory (helped by key phrases jotted in our notebook around which we reconstruct the quote).

Pitman is the classic shorthand system in the UK. It's harder to learn but potentially far faster than the Teeline system. Pitman, which uses symbols to represent sounds (not spellings), is readily capable of 180 wpm and more. At the Mirror scheme, we found that even our best Teeline writers struggled at 130 wpm.

The reason is clear. Teeline also uses symbols, but uses them to represent word abbreviations. For example, the Teeline abbreviation for "Teeline" is formed from the symbols for T, L and N. This is more cumbersome than symbols representing sounds. Teeline, however, has the great merit of being easy to learn and has became the preferred system for journalism.

Curiosity is the greatest freelance virtue. For most outsiders, the skill a journalist needs most is the ability to write. This, however, isn't so. Some say knowledge of politics and economics is the key skill. This has made the Philosophy, Politics and Economics degree at Oxford University popular with intending journalists. Others say a knowledge of people since they are both the source and the stuff of most articles. The late Nicholas Tomalin of the *Sunday Times*, was more cynical. He famously said a journalist most needs "rat-like cunning".

The complete journalist has at least a smattering in all those areas (yes, even the rat-like cunning on occasions) – the freelance even more than the staff person. This is because the freelance has no guaranteed job. He or she is only as good as "the last story but one". (The established freelance will usually be forgiven one duff story!)

However, the most important of all virtues is curiosity, the great driver of journalism. With curiosity – about people, events, situations – we can find a subject buried in the most unpromising material or ask the question that brings to light quite unexpected material. Without curiosity, we'll see only the most obvious stories or simply reproduce what is fed to us by public relations machines.

Curiosity can to some extent be cultivated. As we read press releases, websites, newspapers and magazines, we should constantly ask ourselves *why*, *how* or *what lies behind that*? The same applies as we walk down the street. Many a feature can be picked up by following through on what we see around us.

Three freelance essentials are stamina, unflappability and availability. And the greatest of these is availability. One of the attractions of freelancing is that we aren't tied to a nine-to-five working day. Nor need we work Monday to Friday unless we want to. Most of the time we'll be able to work our commissions around the times and the days we choose to work.

Most commissions aren't "wanted yesterday", but some are. The freelance needs to be ready to accommodate that work even though it breaks into our "me" time, or children's bath time, or quiz night at the pub. Sources, too, have a way of being available only outside our chosen hours. They aren't all sitting in their offices waiting for us to ring them. Perhaps we can only reach that vital source at 10pm at night or on Sunday morning.

Generally speaking, far more time is spent researching a feature article than writing it. That's where stamina and unflappability come in. It takes stamina to track down the people or organisations we want to speak to. When we've done that, it may take many calls or emails – even though the other party is willing – to agree a time for a telephone interview. Then we must repeat the process for others we wish to talk to.

Ideas are the freelance's stock in trade. To find ideas, we need to keep on top of our monitoring of selected newspapers, journals and websites. The flow of new information is relentless. It takes stamina.

Let's imagine a situation where we were commissioned with a deadline a fortnight ahead. With just one day to go, for one reason and another, we still haven't managed to land interviews with two of the four sources we plan to use. Yet we turn in the article on time (having substituted one of the sources with someone more readily available). That's unflappability.

3 GETTING STARTED

Fancy equipment isn't needed. A writer's tools used to consist of pen, ink, paper, desk and chair. Things have moved on, yet not by much. The job will always mean long hours sitting and staring at paper or a screen. Our equipment needn't be fancy, but it's worth getting these basics right.

Get an adjustable, office-style chair with a high back for support. If it swivels, to encourage moments of reflection, so much the better.

A laptop computer is in many ways preferable for the freelance than a PC. It can be used in the office or in the field. And today's large screens and generously sized keyboards mean that a laptop is practicable as our main or only machine.

Unfortunately, they are disastrous for posture. With a laptop we look down at the screen. This puts unwelcome pressure on the upper spine. The recommended position, seen in the arrangement of PCs, is for the eyes to be level with the screen. This keeps the head in a better position.

My personal solution to the laptop dilemma is to use a separate keyboard, which plugs into a USB port, and to raise the laptop on three Yellow Pages directories, good and fat! This home-made solution lifts the screen to the desired position.

Thinking about our chair and our computer is sensible because chronic back pain arising from bad working habits is easier got than got rid of. Sub-editors also face the risk of repetitive strain injuries to the hands, wrists and arms. A writer's use of the keyboard is more intermittent so RSI is less likely. Even so, it's wise to take a screen break for at least a few minutes every hour.

The other items for the office are a telephone, broadband connection, printer, document scanner and camera. We also need an audio recorder for interviews. None of this need be expensive. Standard home-use equipment will be fine for our purposes. Fax is an obsolete but not extinct technology. It will be enough if we have a shop nearby that will send or receive the occasional fax for us; otherwise we need a fax machine.

Apply seat of pants to seat of chair. Freelancing isn't the sort of writing that benefits from our sitting around waiting for inspiration. In fact, except possibly for poetry, it's doubtful whether any writing is. The massive novel output of Charles Dickens and Anthony Trollope (without the help of computers) didn't get written that way!

Most of us need a structure to our working day, and as freelances we have to make our own. There is no recommended best time to write. Some people are at their sharpest in the morning; others in the afternoon or even evening. It also depends on our commitments. Our full-time job may mean we can write only in the evenings and at weekends. Perhaps we have children who are at school during the day, leaving that as the only time to do our freelancing.

Some capacity to make and receive phone calls during weekday daytime is almost certainly necessary, however. This is because we need to be in touch with sources.

If we are at our desks at set times, the ideas and the words will follow. The writing will sometimes go better than at other times. Never mind, get something down rather than nothing. It can always be revised or rewritten later. And our pen, metaphorically, will loosen up as we work.

Distraction is the enemy for the home-based freelance. It's impossible to do our best work with children playing around our feet. Personal phone calls upset the momentum, which may be impossible to regain. It's tempting to attend to minor domestic chores that pop into mind. Hard though it may be, we need to establish work periods that will be free of external interruptions. Many writers have found the answer in the garden shed.

They know about Dr Theatre and Dr Greasepaint in the world of stage and screen. Thanks to these fine doctors, all sorts of illness vanish while the performance is on with the actor remembering he is unwell only when the curtain comes down or the director wraps for the day. As freelances, we can profitably consult Dr Theatre or Dr Greasepaint. They are specialists in aches, pains, colds and fevers. But they would be the last to suggest that we ignore symptoms of more serious illness.

When starting out, bylines are more important than fees. The trickiest placement for a freelance is the first. We have no portfolio of cuttings that we can mention if an editor asks where we've been published before. It's not inevitable that we'll be asked that, but we may be.

This is why it's important to put together a cuttings book. (We should keep this permanently as a record of our career.) Nor should we hang around waiting for the big time. An article in a small newspaper or a minor magazine is worth more than a rejection from a national newspaper! There is no freelancing equivalent of the legendary BA Oxon - failed.

Unsigned articles are fine. Few editors are cynical enough to suspect us of passing off someone else's work as our own. Much better, though, are articles including our byline (ie our name). Bylines are our credentials as writing freelances. They engender confidence not only in editors but also in sources we wish to interview.

In the early stages of freelancing, the byline is more important than the fee. It's a good idea to accept payment at the publication's standard rates (unless the material is truly world-shaking) in the interests of accumulating bylines. Everything is up for negotiation in the freelance world. Although accepting a small fee, we could make it a condition that the article has a prominent byline.

What to do if we are asked about our experience before we've had a single piece published? This is, understandably, the nightmare scenario for beginning freelances. It's unlikely, but the fact that it might happen is an argument for starting lower down the hierarchy and building up a record of work before approaching national newspapers and major consumer magazines.

If we are asked this question, the only way that doesn't dig us in deeper is to be honest. We might say that we have just started as a freelance journalist but are a professional in the area concerned, have contributed to the company intranet, written official reports etc, etc. Most people can come up with something relevant. We are just asking for a chance to show what we can do … Appeal to the Mr Nice Guy or the Ms Friendly in every editor!

Getting published is more important at the start than special copyright terms. National newspapers have elaborate arrangements for selling their material, to counterpart publications around the world, to other papers within Britain and to commercial information archives. Naturally, these syndication activities limit freelances' ability to re-sell the material. We may obtain some further income, but it will be less than if we had re-sold the material ourselves.

Top byliners are so valuable to a newspaper that they are able to make special deals, knowing that they, or their agents, can make more by re-selling directly to other publications. They might, for example, forbid all dissemination apart from the newspaper itself (including the web edition); or exclude certain countries from the syndication.

The byliners start with the whip hand because they own the copyright. But the name, or the material, has to be strong for the newspaper to agree to changing its terms. Most writers are on standard terms for syndication, which is explored further in Chapter 10.

At the start of a freelance career, the priority is to build up a relationship with a chosen publication. This is hardly helped by haggling over copyright so, with the rarest of exceptions, it's better to stick to standard syndication terms.

We have something to offer, but others can offer it too. The upside of freelance journalism is that anyone can do it. The downside is that it sometimes seems that everyone is. We have to believe in ourselves and what we have to offer, but we also have to accept there are others who can offer it too. There are irreplaceable stories but no irreplaceable writers.

Self-belief is one of the ways in which we can stay standing in this crowded field. It will show in how we approach editors and sources. Confidence, which isn't the same as arrogance, usually brings a better outcome than diffidence.

Knowing the subject is a key element in self-belief, underlining the importance of finding the right areas to specialise in. For choice, these will be ones where we have working background or an intense interest as a hobby.

We also need to beware of thinking our rivals have more to offer than we do. They may be looking at us and thinking the same. The reality may be that we are much alike – competent craftspeople. This underlines the importance of building a relationship with a particular publication so the commissioning editor will have no thought of looking elsewhere.

Rejection by one doesn't mean rejection by all. It's tempting, especially in the early days of freelancing, to think that if a proposed article is rejected there's something wrong with it. Tempting but a mistake.

That it's a bad idea is just one of several possibilities, and the one we should put at the bottom of the pile. There may be any number of reasons for rejection that we shan't know about: the commissioning budget is used up; a similar article has already been ordered; the idea isn't right for the particular publication; it's a good idea but not at this time (it lacks a topical peg); the idea has simply been misjudged.

It's unlikely that we'll be told why the article was rejected (editors feel this invites an argument), and *why* doesn't really matter. All that matters is *what* the decision is: yes or no, use it or not. Professional writers move on and look elsewhere. They know that rejection by one publication may be followed by acceptance by another of equal standing.

A case in point was an article I wrote about road plans for Cambridge, one of Britain's most environmentally sensitive cities. This was rejected by the *Guardian* (I never found out why) and accepted in identical form by the *Daily Telegraph*.

It's sensible after a rejection to look again at the idea to see whether it needs to be adjusted or changed. Timing is a particular issue. It may be a good subject, but is it topical at this time?

After, say, three rejections from appropriate publications we should probably accept that the machine won't fly. But perhaps we can bring the idea back in another form or at another time.

A specialism is more profitable than 'across the waterfront' freelancing. Experienced freelances are able to cover any subject required of them from nuclear physics to celebrity fashions. They can do this by asking the right questions and knowing where to find information. However, the reality is that successful freelances have one or two specialisms and stick to those. The science specialist doesn't also handle environment, cookery and sport.

General feature writing is better left to staff journalists who are employed in that role. An "across the waterfront" approach is unpromising for the freelance. There are several reasons for this.

Editors get confused if people offer themselves over too many subjects. We want editors to come to us with commissions, and for that they need a clear idea of what we offer.

A specialist has a greater depth of knowledge than a generalist, giving a crucial edge in the competitive world of freelancing. The specialist becomes known to key sources in the subject, who will tell more than they will to an unknown generalist.

Networking, with contacts and with fellow journalists, is an important activity for freelances. Business cards are a must. We can network effectively in our chosen field, but we can't do so across half a dozen fields.

Columnists are an exception to the rule of specialising (unless they write for special sections like sport and business). They are paid to have an opinion on everything under the sun. Upon examination, we find that they are rarely jobbing journalists. They are senior staff members or celebrities. And often their opinions are quite superficial to anyone who knows about the subject. This doesn't matter. The columnist's brief is to be stimulating, not necessarily profound.

Research the publications covering your chosen field. When we have chosen a subject area in which to write, a first job is to find out the newspapers and magazines in that sector. A trip to the public library remains a more reliable option than searching online. We need to consult *Benn's Media Directory* or *Willings Press Guide*. Both come in three volumes: the UK, Europe and Rest of the World. Each gives a comprehensive list of publications, with contact details.

A list of main newspapers and magazines appears in the famous *Writers' and Artists' Yearbook*. Within the limits of a single volume, the list inevitably isn't comprehensive. In any case, the book should be on every freelance's shelf for its practical advice and legal tips.

It's crucial to know the sales of the titles in our field. The size of the circulation relative to its peer group gives a pretty good indication of a title's success and therefore the competition to place material. The higher the circulation, the more choosy the editors can be. High sales also point to higher fees.

Paid titles in the UK generally belong to the Audit Bureau of Circulations (free publications have separate arrangements for verifying distribution). Without charge, we can search the ABC's website, www.abc.org.uk, to see the sales and distribution of most newspapers and magazines.

If we are starting out, and bearing in mind the first essential is to be published, we sensibly might aim low; if we are an experienced freelance, or someone with marketable knowledge, we should aim higher.

Get to grips with a camera. The rule for freelances has always been, Think Pictures. Feature articles need to be pictorial, and obtaining suitable pictures is a perennial problem for editors. The freelance who can offer pictures alongside the text thus has an advantage. Pictures may make the difference between rejection and acceptance.

In the days of slimmed-down staffs and tight budgets, editors may be unable to assign a staff photographer to the article – another plus for the writer who takes pictures.

Many freelances (including myself) were held back by technical incapacity. Film speeds, shutter speeds and focal length were impenetrable mysteries. But with modern digital cameras, even on the default setting, it's hard *not* to take a technically sound picture.

What's in the picture is another matter. The best camera can't save us from poor composition. Any suggestion of people posing for the camera – either with obviously contrived antics or the opposite, standing stiffly and staring – makes a bad picture.

Crowd scenes where people have their backs to the camera are a common problem. Normally, this is the lazy way although in some countries it's all too understandable: we risk being lynched if we shoot the front!

4 FINDING IDEAS

Most marketable ideas emerge from follow-ups. The follow-up is one of the main techniques of modern journalism. Local newspapers follow up stories from parish magazines, village newsletters and the like. National newspapers follow up from local newspapers and specialist magazines – and from each other.

It works the other way round, too. National announcements may need following up for local newspapers and specialist magazines. Television and radio follow up from national newspapers; less frequently it's the other way round. Everyone follows up press releases.

By the time a story reaches its final national (and international) media incarnation, it will probably be several days old as far as the locals where it originated are concerned!

As freelances, we are part of this elaborate system of follow-ups, or should be. We are more likely to find marketable ideas by searching systematically than by racking our brains in the shower.

The main places we search are other publications, websites and press releases.

Freelances for TV and radio follow an identical routine. The medium is different, but the techniques of journalism are mostly the same.

With hard news of events, products and so on, our target

publication almost certainly will be there before us – perhaps because they have been sent the same press release, or they have found the information themselves, or they have been sent it by the original reporter hoping for an extra fee. We, however, as recommended earlier in the book, are looking for feature subjects. Here we have a realistic prospect of coming up with an idea we can sell.

Read selected publications regularly. In what other job can we read newspapers and magazines, and consider ourselves working! Indeed it's work, and shouldn't be skimped in favour of other, apparently more productive activities. Other publications are a main source of article ideas for us.

If we are writing for the specialist press, we should try to take two daily newspapers, and keep an eye on the websites of some others. If we are writing for the nationals, we should identify the two leading journals in our field and subscribe to them.

There is more traffic from specialist magazines to general newspapers than vice versa. For specialist writers, the magazines are a rich source of stories and article ideas. Nothing captures this better than health, where a plethora of journals headed by the *British Medical Journal* and the *Lancet* meets an insatiable public interest in the subject.

There is nothing magic about the figure two in either case. It's a compromise between searching for information and the time and cost we spend doing so. Newspaper and journal subscriptions can be charged as a business expense, which helps. Our time can't be offset. Most freelances know the need to limit the time spent researching in order to clear the way for interviewing and writing.

Get on the distribution list for press releases. A press release is an announcement that the issuing organisation invites us to use. Most are in the form of news stories, or supposed news stories. Their frequency varies hugely from one a month or even one a year, upwards. A government department may put out two or three on some days.

Press releases are sometimes used as they stand, particularly in smaller magazines. More often, they are taken as the starting point for an article built up by the reporter.

Most press releases are sent by email. The issuers will be happy to include us in their distribution because it costs them nothing. It's sensible not to enlist with too many sources, otherwise we get swamped.

Press releases are useful but need to be treated with care. Organisations can be tempted into quantity rather than quality. The resulting release may contain no real news, or may be rehashing what has been said already.

Statements based on an evaluation or judgment are tricky. "The company was founded in 1958" (which is a plain statement of fact) can be accepted without further checking. "The company is the most successful in the industry" is an evaluation that, for all we know, competitors may dispute. We can use it as a claim by a company official, but we shouldn't state it as a fact without confirming it from a second source.

The Church of England put out a press release about a medieval church stranded in the middle of the Salisbury Plain military training area. It was to be restored by the Churches Conservation Trust. This turned out to be in the "ghost village" of Imber, which was forcibly abandoned in the Second World War and never repopulated. For years the army had been firing all around it, managing to miss the church!

Follow-up inquiries from this not particularly gripping press release gave me a specially provided tour of Imber and news features that I placed with two (non-competing) outlets.

Regularly search selected websites. Where we have chosen not to receive press releases, we can visit websites as required. Most organisations put their press releases on the public website – a development of huge though largely unrecognised significance. For the first time, a company or department can put its exact words before the public without taking out an advertisement or having them filtered by a print journalist or reduced to a soundbite by a broadcaster.

From the journalist's point of view, these are useful statements that might take a long time to obtain by other means. The archive section of the site means we can readily build up background on an organisation.

The essence of searching is *regularity*. When I was the European business correspondent for a Canadian newsletter, I searched sites with different frequencies but with regularity. Major insurers I searched once a week ahead of my weekly filing; I kept an eye on smaller companies and insurance professional bodies once a month. All this was in addition to press releases received directly.

Why not check all sites every day? That wouldn't be an

effective use of time and money if a filing deadline is only weekly; beyond that, as always, we have to strike a balance between the likely value of information and the time taken to obtain it.

Other sections of a website may yield usable information. The annual report, for instance, may contain significant material that isn't helpful to the organisation; hence no press release. These are issued when the organisation has something good to announce, or when something shocking has happened that it needs to respond to. That leaves plenty of stuff in between. Just because it isn't in the press release doesn't mean it isn't news!

Maintain a futures folder. All sorts of continuing stories pop up and are never heard about again, from the council that promises to put in new street lights by the end of the year to the guy travelling from London to Istanbul on a unicycle and planning to get there in August. *Did the council do it? Did the guy make it?*

It's easy to lose track of this forward dimension of stories. We can't depend on the council and the guy telling us. For readers the story is incomplete, and for us as freelances we are missing out on a relatively easy way of earning a further fee. We have done much of the groundwork with the first story.

The futures folder is an effective way to remind ourselves when to look at a story again. It can be a folder in a computer or a physical file. Either way, it will have sub-folders or compartments representing time periods – say, for the months ahead. As each month arrives, we examine the contents of the sub-folder or compartment to see what we need to work on.

A futures folder is more than a note in the diary. Into the folder, as well as a copy of the original article, go associated documents and other material. It then becomes easy to pick up for the new article.

Computers have made it a bit more complicated to operate a futures folder. Documents are likely to be a mixture of digital files and paper material. Unless we are prepared to scan every piece of paper or print out every PDF (neither to be recommended), there isn't anything for it but to have two futures folders, electronic and physical. The old concertina files – an expanding file divided into compartments – have a continuing use.

Ask yourself whether the article has a topical peg. Lord Northcliffe, an important figure in the history of journalism, said this about features: "There are two main divisions of news: one, actualities, two talking points. The first is news in its narrowest and best sense – reports of happenings, political resignations, strikes, crimes, deaths of famous people, wrecks and railway smashes, weather storms, sporting results, and so on. The second is getting the topics people are discussing and developing them, or stimulating a topic oneself…

"News of the second sort, the 'talking points', the 'features', is news that does not fall into your basket like the other sort. It requires thought, initiative, looking ahead. It means … a daily search for subjects in the public mind, or subjects that ought to be in the public mind. There are some who say it is this second sort of news, these 'features', and 'talking points', that sells the newspapers. I do not agree. It is hard news that catches readers. Features hold them." [Quoted by Tom Clarke in *My Northcliffe Diary*]

This distinction between news and features remains readily recognisable today, a century later – nowhere more than in the newspaper he founded, the *Daily Mail*. Features usually look different from news articles; perhaps they are presented in a separate section. But Northcliffe reminds us that *the best features grow out of news*.

A strong topical peg may make the difference between acceptance and rejection of our idea. The best time to write about Caesarean sections is when the latest annual figures provide a peg to hang the article on. Controversial subjects from fox hunting to road pricing are bubbling away below the surface all the time. Some news *raison d'etre* is needed to make a marketable article.

There are published features that fail this test. They are the worse for it. Hopefully, we don't write them. We should ask ourselves this about our idea: could the article have run three months ago, or could it run next year, in the same form? If the answer is yes, we should look for a topical peg to make the article right for here and now.

Observation and curiosity have a role. An exercise beloved of journalism trainers and editors is to send the student or new recruit for a walk with instructions to come back with five feature ideas. They are right.

At a more professional level, we can use the same approach. We're unlikely simply to fall over a news story, but features, being chiefly about continuing issues, can be created from the raw materials that we see around us. Observation and curiosity are part of the freelance's toolkit along with a sense of topicality (see previous section).

We spend a weekend in the country. On a walk, we find the fieldpath ploughed up in places while farther on a gate has been nailed shut. Why do farmers do this? Who is responsible for enforcing public rights of way? What are the problems of enforcement? How many staff? How much budget? Is the problem getting worse or better? What about badly behaved walkers, who trample on crops and leave gates open so that livestock get out? Are there too many public rights of way, given that most are little used? Is the opposite true: that people should be able to walk anywhere over land not under crops? What is the experience of countries where they can? And so on.

From a simple personal experience several approaches to a worthwhile feature can be found.

The village where we are staying has no shop, but we notice not one but two supermarket delivery vans. Does this mean villagers are no longer stranded for food shopping? How many supermarkets come into the village? Who uses the service, and who doesn't? Is it only for the well-to-do? Do you have to order via the internet? What do villagers think of shopping this way? How big must a village be to support a food shop? What will happen in the future to village shops? Are community owned and staffed shops a serious option? What difference does a post office make to the economics of a village shop? And so on.

Again, from observation we can develop worthwhile feature ideas with a topical twist on an important social issue.

These are examples of an approach that can be used anywhere. Having found a subject, we spin off as many questions as we can. Then we chuck most of them away, leaving us with a specific angle or theme for the feature.

Call on contacts. Everyone we have talked or written to in a working situation is a potential contact for the future. Provided we haven't fallen out with them, we can call on them to help us with the next article. And the next... In that sense, research becomes easier as we build up a network of sources.

This thought comes with a note of caution: we should be open at all times to expanding and renewing the network. Probably we can all think of cases in the media where the same old names come up on the same old subjects. Journalists call these people, derisively, "rent-a-quotes". The people we should be deriding when we always reach for the obvious source are ourselves. It's sloppy journalism.

Contacts are part of a freelance's stock in trade so we should keep a careful note – in a book or computer file or on index cards – of those who may be useful in the future plus their areas of specialism. It will also be useful to record when we last had contact with them.

When the article has appeared, it's polite to send the contact a cutting and a line of thanks. It's worth being meticulous about this as an investment in future good relations.

It's an unfortunate fact of life that no-one phones with information unless they are flogging something or puffing something. Yet if we approach the contact, a worthwhile tip or lead may be volunteered. So, the more we meet our contacts the better – at conferences, social occasions, even by phoning them periodically for a chat. Information obtained in these ways may well be exclusive, or at least ahead of an official announcement, giving the freelance a valuable beat on the news.

The most valuable contact details are people's mobile and home telephone numbers. These mean that we can expect to get them at all times, not just in office hours, bypassing personal assistants and other gatekeepers. Exactly for that reason, these numbers can be hard to get. One way is to ask at the end of an interview how we can contact the person for follow-up queries over the next 48 hours. This approach works particularly well on Friday afternoons!

Factual information is more marketable than opinions. Facts are the gold standard of journalism. This applies to features as much as to news. Features are interpretative or opinion-based, but they are based on facts. If the feature is to work, there will be new facts, informative facts or unusual facts.

Like truffles, facts are valuable because of the difficulty and time involved in rooting them out. It's easy to fill space in a newspaper or magazine with opinion pieces, where the writer can waffle to whatever length is needed. The market in such pieces is correspondingly weak unless we are a "name" or an expert.

The best prospects for the working freelance are factually based news features, either on topical issues or personal experiences (reinforced with factual backgrounding). As journalism has become more personal and celebrity-based, we do well to quarry our own lives for experiences that might interest the wider world. Health and survival (or both) have a constant appeal.

Facts can be slippery customers. We can state that *Paris is the capital of France* without qualification or fear of contradiction. To say that *mercury in dental fillings is below the level that threatens human health* reads like a factual statement, but is no such thing. The toxicity of mercury in amalgam has been disputed for 150 years. The controversy is unlikely to be settled anytime soon.

The statement cries out to be qualified, along the lines of *the mainstream view is that mercury in dental fillings presents no threat to human health,* or *mercury in dental fillings is generally held to present no threat to human health.*

It can be hard to spot these factual time-bombs when we are given information from an authoritative source. I remember coming to grief 40 years ago over fluoride in the water supply – an issue that is still with us. But we can develop a nose for controversial information. One person's fact may be another person's lie, which is a hazard that journalists face every working day.

5   COMMISSIONS

Commissions are the goal for freelances. Before they put pen to paper, or fingers on keyboard, established freelances expect to be commissioned. That is also the goal for all freelances. A commission is an order for a piece of work, which should specify at minimum (a) what the article is to be about, (b) the fee, (c) when it's to be submitted, (d) how long it should be and (e) the rights being acquired – ie the copyright, meaning that the writer has no control over or financial interest in the piece, or more limited rights.

In practice, commissions for long-standing freelances are often given by word of mouth rather than in writing. Charming as this is in its way, the practice isn't recommended. Even among friends, there may be disagreements later about what was ordered – and nothing on paper to say who is right.

Commissions that don't give enough detail about what is wanted may give problems later. "Airport expansion issues" is useless as guidance to the writer. What particular aspect – planning, economic, human, climatic – are we to pursue? Which airports? We should be sure at the outset that the brief is sufficiently detailed. If it isn't, then is the time to ask for clarification.

A commission isn't the same as being told that a publication will look at our article, although editors complain that enthusiastic beginning freelances often confuse the two. A commission is a contract, and as such it imposes certain obligations on the commissioning editor (explained later in this chapter). Being invited to submit an article imposes no obligations other than the moral one of giving fair consideration to the material sent in.

An unknown freelance, whether beginning or established, can't expect to be commissioned from the start. We have to go through the stage of sending in our work speculatively. Being invited to submit an article is in itself an achievement. Editors don't waste time and effort in saying they will look at something unless there is a possibility it will suit.

Nevertheless, the goal is for editors to come to us with commissions, or for us to suggest articles that are then commissioned. We offer editors ideas, which we work up into articles only after some expression of interest, either a commission or an invitation to submit.

Famous writers can get away with it, but the rest of us should avoid submitting complete articles speculatively. This is a badge of amateurism.

A commissioning letter avoids problems later. A written (email or paper) commission is a sensible precaution against future misunderstandings about what was ordered. Perhaps it's surprising that all commissions aren't put in writing. A busy editorial department issues thousands a year, and hard-pressed staff may yield to the temptation of telling someone on the phone. Yet the need for commissioning letters is greater now than ever, with great variations in the rights being bought (the copyright or less than the copyright).

The nightmare scenario for a freelance is for the commissioning editor to be suddenly purged, and no letter. Then there is nothing to stop the new editor, by accident or design, denying that there is a commission. Unfortunately, this is a common scenario. Incoming editors often want to bring in new ideas and new writers. They want to get rid of as many prior obligations as they can.

If we have failed to obtain a commissioning letter, it's a good idea to send a letter ourselves stating what we understand the commission to be, including subject and fee. This will have some value in the event of a disagreement, although less than a commissioning letter. It should be sent by email so that the date and time are shown. Better still will be if it generates a read receipt (proving that the email was received and opened).

Give minimum information in an outline. We may be asked to provide an outline (also known as a scenario). This is so that the editor can evaluate the proposed article and decide whether to commission it.

An outline is a short note setting out the subject of the article and how it will be developed – sources, published reports and so on – with the proposed length. It will be useful to mention the topical peg that is the *raison d'etre* for the article. If pictures are available, that may help to win the commission.

Here is a typical outline for a news feature:

Newest figures out on social problem of village shop closures. Article asks whether community-run shops are the answer, and focuses on village shop trading successfully for six years. Interviews with shop manager, octogenarian customer and business association official (for national scene), plus background reports. Proposed length: 800 words. Pictures available.

This outline is short (50 words), and is specific without giving details. It doesn't identify the village or the relevant trade association, or even the source of the "newest figures" on shop closures. However, it gives enough for the editor to evaluate the proposal.

Detailed information is part of our trading capital as freelances. The aim of an outline is to provide minimum necessary information: enough to win the commission but not so much that someone else can lift our idea. Theft of ideas isn't widespread in journalism, but it does happen. Cash-strapped editors have been tempted to use writers on payroll for articles originating with freelances, thereby saving the freelance fee.

We can never prove that the idea didn't occur to the editor independently of us, but we can minimise the risk of our idea being purloined.

Expect to be asked for rewrites, in magazines more than in newspapers. When we have submitted a commissioned article, that isn't necessarily the last we hear of it until publication. The newspaper or magazine may ask for further material or even a rewrite in whole or part. It's important not to take this personally. If world-famous authors can have their scripts rejected by Hollywood, what's a little rewriting for a magazine!

The publication may have good reason to require these changes that are nothing to do with the competence of the writer. It may want a different take on the subject (was the initial briefing detailed enough?), other articles that the writer can know nothing about may affect the situation, the news climate may have changed since the article was commissioned.

Evidence from contributors to my freelancing column over the years shows that consumer magazines are more likely to demand rewrites than national newspapers. In other words, the glossies at the top end pay as well as national newspapers, but the writers have to sweat for it!

It may be that the magazines have more time to work on the material or, coming out less frequently, are more concerned to get it perfect. Perhaps it's down to the temperament of those who work on newspapers and magazines, or simply a tradition of heavier sub-editing on newspapers (so that changes are made in the office, not by the freelance). In any case, it's better to grit our teeth and get on with it. And, of course, the changes might even be an improvement.

All these comments apply to commissioned pieces. It's unlikely that we'll be asked to rewrite an article sent on spec. It will be either accepted or rejected.

A commissioned article that isn't used should be paid in full. Articles are commissioned and not used for several reasons. Features, almost as much as news, need topicality. If the news changes and the feature is no longer topical, it won't be used. Some publications regularly over-commission in an attempt to ensure an unfailing supply of high grade material, meaning that many articles will never get in. An editor may have had a change of heart, or have been replaced by someone with different ideas.

None of these rejections is the writer's fault. He or she has done the work as commissioned, and is entitled to be paid for it. The publishing industry has recognised this for years by paying in full for an article thus discarded.

Unfortunately, recent years have seen the spread of "kill fees", often just 50% of the commissioned amount. This is an alien growth imported from the film industry (where fees are much higher so that 50% of a lot is still a lot!). We should squawk if we're asked to accept a kill fee and politely point out that for decades this hasn't been best publishing practice.

If the article is in some way sub-standard, that's a different matter. We shouldn't expect to be paid for something we haven't delivered. Even in this, hopefully rare, situation, the idea of a kill fee has difficulties. Unless the material is so time-sensitive that it won't stand over to the next day, we are entitled to expect a chance to put things right. That way the article becomes publishable, and payable, again.

Articles may be sub-edited without the writers' moral rights being infringed. The Copyright, Designs and Patents Act 1988 sets out a system of moral rights to protect writers and other producers of creative work. This is why we see statements like "The moral rights of the author have been asserted" in books.

Among the most important is the *integrity right* prohibiting an author's work from being subject to "derogatory treatment" in the editing process. Newspapers and magazines saw that, at least in the eyes of super-sensitive writers, this would make active sub-editing of copy impossible! So periodical publications are exempted from this provision of the copyright act.

We may not care for it but, unlike a book author, we can't complain if that gem of a first paragraph is lost, the finer points of our argument removed or that compelling quote dropped! It's better to stay positive. The perfect sub-editor has yet to emerge, but wise writers accept that sub-editors improve more than they spoil.

In fact, the charge against sub-editors in this era of stripped-down staffs is that they do too *little* to copy. Mistakes of spelling, grammar, fact, taste and emphasis, which ought to have been caught, sail into print. That is the case with newspapers and many magazines. The top-end glossies are heavily into altering copy, but it tends to be the writer who is asked to do it.

More philosophically, we need to reflect that an article isn't a personal product in the same way as a book or a poem. It may have our name on it, but ultimately the article is our contribution to the team effort, which is the newspaper or magazine.

Steady relationships with a few publications are more profitable than promiscuously writing for all and sundry. Freelancing conjures up visions of the writer publishing, here, there and everywhere. The reality is that successful freelances have a limited number of outlets. It's more productive to build strong and lasting relationships with two or three publications than to cover the waterfront.

It's no accident that well known byliners – many of whom will be freelances – don't appear regularly in more than two or three publications.

Remember that we want editors to approach us with commissions. They are more likely to do that if we're well known to them. We want them to be receptive to our article pitches. That's less likely if we are unknown to them.

The happy medium can be hard to strike. We need also to beware of the opposite trap, of depending on a single client. It's very tempting when the money and the placements are regular; it's also very hazardous. We would be like an employee but with few of the protections of an employee.

It only needs the editor or the policy to change, and we have lost our income. Both are common experiences in journalism. An incoming commissioning editor often marks out his or her territory by purging the existing roll of contributors. Editors are prone to enthusiasms, not all of which may be entirely rational. That's part of what makes them creative. So policy, and the sort of material needed, may change in a blink.

Fifty per cent is the golden rule. As freelances, we try to steer between the clashing rocks of having a single client, which makes us their captive, and having too many, which means we probably don't make our mark with any. The optimum number of regular writing outlets is probably two or three, but more important is the income situation.

The golden rule of freelancing isn't to let a single client account for more than 50% of net earnings, provided that the remaining 50% leaves enough to live on. This means that the loss of no one client can hole us below the waterline – an essential state of affairs if we're in freelancing for the long term.

The rule refers to "net earnings" – ie after business expenses – because gross earnings can give a misleading picture. We might decide to cut down on a useful client because earnings seem to breach the 50% rule and we fear over-dependency. However, those jobs include substantial travel and the client pays for this. Subtracting these travel expenses, we find that net fees are less than half the total. We can happily keep working for that client.

The golden rule should be interpreted as 50% of all earnings – ie what we have to live on – rather than 50% of income from freelance articles. We should take into account staple jobs like sub-editing shifts and lecturing, or even work outside journalism. It's fine economically (although not necessarily desirable) for one client to produce 75% of the income from freelance articles when articles account for only 50% of our income. In that example, the dominant writing client accounts for only 37.5% of total income.

If losing one client means we shan't have enough to live on, that's a wake-up signal to broaden our economic base, either by finding more writing clients or by taking other jobs inside or outside journalism.

Don't be shy about asking for expenses. Those that don't ask don't get. Editors may reimburse certain of the costs we incur in researching an article – but are unlikely to volunteer the payment. It's up to us to ask. The time to do this is when the article is being commissioned, not after we've written it. Editors dislike *faits accomplis*, and may refuse the request.

The evidence from numerous freelances suggests that editors are often surprisingly liberal with expenses, but only if they are signalled in advance.

The main expenses in writing a feature are phone calls, travel and meals when fieldwork is involved, and perhaps the cost of reports and documents.

Routine phone calls are part of a freelance's business overhead, and we shouldn't expect to reclaim them. International calls have become so cheap that it's hard to make out an expenses case. If we interview someone on a mobile phone in Australia, that would be a significant cost that we could hope to claim.

With so much material available free on the internet, it's hard to make a case for buying reports and documents. There may be times, however, when we have to shell out £25 for a report, and we should try to have that repaid as expenses.

Travel and meals when on fieldwork are usually the main element of expenses. As freelances, we are expected to absorb small travel costs – for the London-based freelance, journeys in the central zones with an Oyster pre-pay card, for example – but we can hope for expenses with longer journeys. A train trip from London to Oxford to interview a professor is certainly worth claiming. For car trips, discover the publication's mileage rate and claim that. To find out the length of trip in advance, the route planner tool on www.theaa.co.uk is valuable and free.

It looks better to ignore minor food items like mid-morning coffee in an expenses claim. Lunch is normally allowable at the sandwich bar or pasta house level.

Sometimes expenses requests will be turned down, but more often they are allowed. Either way, we don't lose face, or somehow seem cheap, by asking. We'll seem businesslike. The more receipts we provide, particularly train tickets and meal bills, the more likely the claim is to go through without challenge.

6 APPROACHING EDITORS

Discover who commissions material in our subject area. About the least useful person on a national newspaper to pitch a feature to is ... the features editor. This lofty personage does little day-by-day commissioning. The role is devolved to journalists in charge of the various desks, sections, pages and offshoots (like magazines and supplements) known as commissioning editors. These are the people we need to reach.

A national newspaper has an enormous number of people with the authority to commission articles – 30 or more desk and section heads together with deputies. It's the same story on a smaller scale with the larger national magazines. Only with local newspapers and small magazines is the "features editor" as such, or someone answering to that name, the right person to pitch to.

When trying to place an article, it's essential to contact the right person. The wrong person will say no thanks, and is very unlikely to suggest someone else to try. The same idea pitched to the right person might have secured a yes.

Close scrutiny of our target publication is the best way to discover the best section or page to aim at, even if it isn't obvious who commissions in those areas (see next heading).

On the largest newspapers, an article may potentially fit more than one part of the paper – for example, the main feature section, a special page, the magazine, a supplement; perhaps even separate publication in the web edition.

That's why we need to be clear where we are going. It also means we have several selling possibilities within the single publication. We can bicycle our idea around the various parts without embarrassment. Staff are far too busy to notice!

Commissioning editors complain that freelances don't do enough research before making a pitch. From the stories they tell, they clearly have a point.

If you can't find out way who commissions material in your subject area, ask the switchboard. It's helpful to know the name of the commissioning editor of the section we are approaching. This isn't always easy.

For the larger newspapers, internal directories may give complete lists of commissioning editors, but these are hard to get hold of. In any case, they rapidly become out of date as the hot seat becomes part of the game of musical chairs.

Some magazines helpfully print substantial lists of editors in their mastheads (the inside box with identifying details of the publication). Otherwise, it's down to detective work.

It may be obvious from the page itself who the commissioning editor is because they often write, too.

Someone bylined "science editor" will most likely have commissioning authority for science articles.

If all else fails, we can ring up and ask the switchboard. We should say "I'd like to know please the name of the person in charge of..." or something similar. The term "commissioning editor" is better avoided. The operator may not understand it.

We may be taken for cold-calling salesman, but never mind: the switchboard is unlikely not to tell us. Operators don't sit in judgment on calls. In fact, in media they daren't. That unknown caller may have the scoop of the century. To turn the call away would be a disaster.

Phone rather than email to pitch an idea to a new client. New freelances wake up in the night terrified of it. Veteran writers find a knot in their stomach. Even correspondents back from a war zone shake a little as they pick up the phone.

The object of their fears is cold-calling an unknown editor to pitch an idea. It's surely one of the toughest jobs for journalists, who in the main aren't natural salespeople for their own wares.

Who needs the constant voicemails, the hassle of getting past PAs and, above all, the fear of rejection? The answer is, we all do with a potential new client.

Sometimes it seems there is a culture among commissioning editors of ignoring emails and, even more, letters. Probably it's down to inefficiency and being swamped with emails. Certainly we're more likely to get a satisfactory result if we pick up the phone and go live.

By talking on the phone the editor gets a better sense of what's on offer and, crucially, is able to infer things about the stranger who is offering it. We may be able to turn a lukewarm reaction into a positive response. Without this contact, even if we get a reply to our email it's likely to be in default mode – no.

Of course, we may not get through. We may run repeatedly

up against the voicemail or encounter a secretary guarding the boss like a dragon at the gate. If this happens, we can at least send an email referring to the attempted contact. That email will be on a stronger footing than one sent out of the blue.

If we speak to the editor and the answer is no thanks, we should take the opportunity of asking whether he or she can think of other parts of the publication that might be interested.

Before making the phone call, it's a good idea to jot down the three or four points we wish to make. We should also practise our opening remarks. Impressions are formed in the first few seconds. We only get one shot at this.

Contacting existing clients is quite another matter. We are in a relationship with them. They know us and our work. In those circumstances an email is usually the preferred way of pitching an idea.

Don't leave an idea lying around: 'use it or lose it'. One of the biggest complaints of freelances is about editors who don't say yes and don't say no to a proposed feature article. Sadly, there are a lot of these editors around.

Because the most marketable material is strongly topical, sitting on an idea and finally saying no means the idea can't be sold elsewhere. The answer isn't to pitch the article in several places at once. What if they all say yes? We then have the embarrassment of telling people that they can't have it after all – hardly a prescription for good future relations.

The aim is to offer feature ideas to outlets consecutively, but to get answers quickly enough so that, if necessary, the piece can be offered elsewhere.

How quickly we need an answer depends on who we are aiming at. Generally speaking, the shelf life of an idea is shorter than we might think. All manner of hot issues, from health foods and GPs' pay to car taxes and size zero, are of interest to leading publications only with a news peg to hang them on.

For a daily newspaper the publication window is days, not weeks. In this situation, we need an answer to our proposal within 48 hours at most.

A monthly magazine will typically move more slowly. A decision may not be possible immediately because the rest of the contents haven't been assembled. These include rival claimants to the space our article might occupy. The freelance's reaction will depend on the deadlines for the publications that might be approached next. Like the hourly bus service, there's a long time to wait if we miss the deadline. By that time the idea will be out of date.

Anything between 24 hours and one week, depending on individual cases, is a reasonable time to keep ideas for appraisal. Beyond that, the article is stuck in the system and may never emerge of its own accord. We should start pressing, and if necessary withdraw the idea in order to offer it elsewhere.

Commissioning editors recognise that article ideas are a perishable commodity. They won't be offended if, politely but firmly, we press them for a decision.

Offer pictures. We should offer photographs with our articles even if we make no claim to be a photographer. Features need to be illustrated, and the commissioning editor may not have the budget to assign a professional photographer. The availability of pictures from another source may make the difference between acceptance and rejection of a proposal.

The subject of the article may have suitable stock shots or perhaps will arrange photos especially for our article. No payment should be made for this material, even if asked for: the subject is already benefitting from the publicity (otherwise they wouldn't have agreed to be interviewed), and that is reward enough. In many cases, however, we can take acceptable pictures ourselves using a simple digital camera.

These cameras take "aim and shoot" to a new level of accomplishment. Even the default setting will normally be enough to secure a publishable picture, handy for dummies like myself. We don't have to think about exposure; we do have to think about aim.

A bit of leeway in a picture is a good thing: to come in too tightly around the subject of the picture is unhelpful, whether that be a person or a scene. The picture editor can crop content to the shape and emphasis required but can't put back what isn't there.

Feature articles are exclusive to your particular client in their market. News reports are sold non-exclusively unless an arrangement is made to the contrary, meaning that correspondents send them simultaneously to as many outlets as they please. Feature articles, by contrast, are exclusive even though nothing is likely to be said in the commissioning letter.

The difference lies in the personalisation and interpretation that one finds in a feature – elements that are limited or non-existent in a news story. Obviously the *Guardian* doesn't want to run the same feature as the *Independent*, or as the *Times* or the *Daily Telegraph* for that matter. The readership of these newspapers overlap to a greater or lesser extent.

Note, however, that the popular papers – what used to be called the tabloids – cheerfully reprint features that have already appeared in one of the "unpopulars". They know that any readership overlap is too small to worry about. (Incidentally, it's an interesting illustration of how the writing styles of the "rags" and the "qualities" aren't as different as usually supposed. Much of the difference is in the typographical display.)

An editor would feel seriously aggrieved if, by accident, the same feature appeared in a competitor. The editor can't know what else has been done with the material. The onus is on the freelance not to sell the same piece twice to competing outlets.

This isn't to say that the same piece can't be sold to non-competing outlets (eg a regional magazine vis a vis a national newspaper) or that a different piece can't be constructed from the same underlying material. Both are possible in the right circumstances – the subject of the next two headings.

Look for ways to place material more than once. Old hands like to say "A piece isn't sold until it's been sold four times". While this is a counsel of perfection, it's a useful reminder to work our material to the uttermost. Most freelances don't do this because they aren't aware of the possibilities of the law of copyright.

It was noted above that mass market national newspapers commonly pick up pieces from the upmarket papers. These deals are normally arranged between the newspapers, but the freelance writer will often get a share of the proceeds of selling on.

Re-publication in another sector of the marketplace is a simple way to earn a further fee. A sale might be made to a magazine, a regional newspaper or a web service. Whether we are free to seek a further sale like this depends on the rights we have sold to the original publisher. We need to know the copyright status.

An article sold to a regional newspaper, say the *Yorkshire Post*, may be sold simultaneously to a regional in another part of the country, say the *Evening Post* (Bristol), without breaching exclusivity. Or indeed to several such regionals. This is because their circulation areas don't overlap.

Don't use up all your ammunition on one target. More than one piece may be constructed from the same material. We can sell the second piece even if we have sold the copyright to the first piece (and can do nothing more with it). *How* different the pieces need to be to become separate articles depends on where we are placing them.

For two national newspapers, even if not directly competing, anything more than the same broad subject might be difficult. For a national newspaper and a national consumer magazine, the overlap could be quite extensive. The topic is examined in more detail in Chapter 10, dealing with copyright.

This approach means not using up all our ammunition on the first target. Having something left over for a second article applies over time, too. For example, we have interviewed sources and assembled background facts on the perennial subject of NHS funding of expensive drugs. Some of this information might find itself in an article six months later, when a new peg arises. Additional work would be minimal, although we would need a quick check with our sources for any updates – and to make sure that none had died. The more time goes by, the greater the risk of quoting a dead person as still alive!

When an article has run, ask about writing more. A one-off placing in a good publication makes a useful entry in our cuttings file, but it doesn't do much to build a freelance career. The aim is to use this piece as a bridgehead to write further articles.

Unlike Oliver Twist, the freelance who asks for more may well get a positive result. Certainly, it's more likely than by sitting at home waiting for the phone to ring. The article means a lot to us but it's one among many for the busy commissioning editor. He or she isn't spending time thinking, "What else can I use that talented Jane ---- (or John ----) on?"

The best time to ask about writing more articles is directly after a piece has appeared. Get through by phone if possible. We can't expect a single article to be followed by commissions or even requests to see material speculatively. Both of those will follow later. What we are looking for is a listening ear for our own ideas.

Once we have been told that more ideas are welcome, we should follow up within a few days. Two article proposals, or three at most, are enough. Bombarding editors with more than that looks too eager, and may put them off.

Our suggestions should each comprise a couple of sentences of description together with the statement "Full outline available if required". There is a defensive reason for this caution. We don't want to give away too much about articles if we aren't going to be asked to write them.

7 RESEARCHING

Researching an article is likely to take more time than writing it. For researched features – that is the type of article where we have several quoted sources and extensive factual background – the bulk of the time is likely to be spent on getting the material together.

It's possible to give a "par for the course" time with writing; it isn't possible with researching. Material varies enormously in how long it takes to get. Interviews, for example, take longer or shorter to set up and quite properly vary in length; background may be easily available or we may have to hunt for it.

A good benchmark of writing speed is 300 words an hour, or a little more. That said, no-one should worry if they write more slowly. (If they write a lot faster, they should ask themselves whether the writing is suffering in the rush.)

Writers vary enormously in their natural pace of writing. Some consider 750 words to be a day's work. On the other hand, Henry Morton Stanley, the legendary African explorer who did everything by extremes, assembled the blockbuster accounts of his travels at the rate of 8,000 words a day!

There are exceptions to this idea that researching takes up more time than writing. A personal column where we have the facts at our fingertips, a celebrity profile consisting mainly of what she said in an interview and reworking existing material to make a second article are all cases in point.

Most of our work isn't likely to be that straightforward, however. Since time is money for the professional freelance, we have to ensure that we don't become trapped in too much research.

We can never get to the end of a subject. Particularly with the coming of the internet, there is so much information out there that we can't hope to get to the end of our subject, whether that is a person, a company or an issue. It may be helpful in finding our way through this jungle of information to reflect that we aren't writing an Encyclopedia Britannica entry.

In other words, we can't hope to say it all. Nor need we carry the weight of producing a definitive account that will stand for years. We just do the best we can with the tools at our disposal. (Come to think of it, even Encyclopedia Britannica writers must accept that they can't say it all, and aren't infallible!)

A key pointer to what to include and what to leave out is *target readership* – who the article is written for. For example, an article about trends in packaging would have different background if written for supermarket managers rather than for the general public.

We also need to be hard-nosed and weigh the time to be taken on research against the financial return. If I'm being paid £1,000 for an article I can afford to do more research than if I'm to be paid £200. The £200 article will still need adequate backgrounding and sourcing, but the commissioning editor for the £1,000 article will, quite properly, expect something with a bit extra.

Be clear what you want from your research. We can reduce the time spent on research by being clear before we start about what we want. One aspect of this is to decide how many people we wish to interview and quote. How do we get hold of them? How tough will it be to set up the interview? If it's difficult, is this source vital or can we move on to someone else?

We can decide at the outset which areas of background to include and which to leave out. That's not to say that if an unexpected and interesting point comes along we shouldn't follow it, but in general fishing expeditions aren't time-effective.

How much biodata on our interviewees do we need? Perhaps nothing at all beyond their present jobs. On the other hand, if someone has an unusual history – worked in many countries perhaps – it would be worth finding out more about that.

In the article on Caesarean sections referred to earlier in this book, we might decide not to investigate the history of this operation (which goes back centuries) or mortality over the years (which was huge for the mother until recent times). Nor are we interested in how the operation is performed.

All of these are interesting topics, but for our article they are byeways down which we shouldn't wander. Our focus is on why it has become so widespread, particularly who is driving the process – the patients or the doctors.

Like the bricklayer who doesn't want to build the wall in the wrong place or to the wrong height, time spent in planning research is likely to be recouped many times over.

Beware undated information from search engines. Web pages that come up on internet searches may be years old, and they aren't always dated. The first rule of using web pages for research is always check for the date. The second rule is if the date isn't known, beware of the information.

Using undated information for any but the most straightforward geographical and historical information is hazardous. The height above sea level of the city of Nairobi, Kenya (5,450ft or 1,660m) and the date of the Battle of Marston Moor (1644) are unlikely to change. Beyond that, most undated information needs substantiating. Even if the page is from a reliable source, later information may have turned the situation upside down.

The Google search engine has a valuable service in Google News. This picks up news reports from hundreds of publications around the world, ranked either by relevance to the search words (default mode) or date. This material clearly is up to date and is helpful for recent factual information. It uses news reports, not official sites, so isn't authoritative for background. We also need to be careful that in making use of this information we aren't recycling the mistakes of other journalists.

'Fair dealing' allows us to quote copyright material. Most of the printed material that we want to quote will be subject to copyright, meaning that there are restrictions on its use. Copyright in the UK lasts for a long time – during an author's lifetime and for 70 years after his or her death.

Hence the work of such legendary Victorian writers as Thomas Hardy and Rudyard Kipling only relatively recently came into the public domain. With unsigned newspaper articles and reports, the restricted period is 70 years from the date of publication.

Nor does copyright apply only where we see the © symbol. It's inherent in all written work (as well as other forms of intellectual property like paintings and photographs).

The good news for writers is that provided we use common sense we can quote from copyright material without fear of being in breach of the law. We musn't quote too much (see next section) and must attribute the source. If we do this, we enjoy the protection of *fair dealing*.

This is a legal concept set out in the Copyright, Designs and Patents Act 1988, Section 30, dealing with criticism, review and news reporting:

(1) Fair dealing with a work for the purpose of criticism or review, of that or another work or of a performance of a work, does not infringe any copyright in the work provided that it is accompanied by a sufficient acknowledgement.
(2) Fair dealing with a work (other than a photograph) for the purpose of reporting current events does not infringe any copyright in the work provided that (subject to subsection (3)) it is accompanied by a sufficient acknowledgement.

The act doesn't spell out what is a sufficient acknowledgement, but by general practice we need the title and the author when quoting from a book. The publisher may be added if desired. Quoting from a report, we should give at least the title and the name of the organisation issuing it. A newspaper or magazine article should identify at least the publication and, according to context, the writer and possibly the headline.

I don't think the date of publication is essential in any of these cases, unless leaving it out affects the matter being quoted. Including the date may be desirable journalistically, however.

Word limits for quotes are generous. The Copyright, Designs and Patents Act 1988 doesn't spell out how much quotation amounts to too much, or "unfair dealing".

> *A useful industry benchmark is 300 words maximum of verbatim quotation of a single passage, and 800 words maximum from the work being quoted, always provided that the quoted material does not amount to more than 25% of the whole.*

Eight hundred words quoted from a 100,000-word book is obviously a different matter from 800 words out of a 1,600-word article, hence the limitation of one quarter.

While these limits may concern book writers – who need to get permission from the copyright holder to quote more – they are more than any journalist is likely to need. Direct quotations aren't a problem for us so long as we follow the ground rules.

Non-verbatim quotations, ie paraphrases, may be even more extensive, but we need to be careful that we aren't quoting so much as to affect the commercial value of the original. We would be unwise to paraphrase the entire conclusions of a newly published book, making it unnecessary for anyone to spend £20 on the original.

The copyright holder can give permission for the material to be quoted in any amounts. This is what happens when newspapers serialise books. The extracts are so extensive that one wonders why anyone would buy the original. Perhaps few do. The publisher doesn't care (although the author does), having made the money from the serialisation fee.

Press releases are an area where we can quote freely without reference to word limits. In fact, the producers will be delighted if we use their material as it stands. A press release comes with an implied copyright consent to use the content.

Use the techniques of journalistic interviewing. Effective use of our sources depends on successful interviewing. This is a learnt technique with very little in common with casual questions in conversation. The interviewer has a clear idea of the ground he or she wishes to cover while remaining open to unexpected points that come along.

Above all, we must be good listeners. The interrupter is unlikely to get to the bottom of a situation, and in any event will take twice as long! Interviews are usually best begun with a general, *omnibus question* on the lines of "Please would you describe in a nutshell what happened" or "Please can you tell me in outline about your plans" and so on. This approach usually draws out the essence of a situation, after which we start more detailed questions.

The best reporters don't go storming into a situation with size 12 boots. They seem to be chatting to the interviewee, jollying them along with a softly softly approach.

In adversarial interviews, tough questions can be put without offence using the Spenlow and Jorkins method. Mr Jorkins, in Dickens's *David Copperfield*, was a "mild man" whose role in the firm "was to keep himself in the background, and be constantly exhibited as the most obdurate and ruthless of men" – allowing Mr Spenlow to say no and blame it on someone else.

The journalistic equivalent is "How do you answer critics who say you've run the company into the ground/have been in the job too long/are a heartless axeman?" and so on.

The question "Can I quote you?" belongs only in Hollywood films of a certain period. It positively invites the interviewee to say no! In a formal interview situation, permission to use what is said is implicit. It's up to the interviewee to put remarks off the record, not up to us to put them on the record.

At informal encounters particularly with ordinary people not used to dealing with the media, we proceed indirectly by saying something like "That's very interesting. I want to use that in my article", followed by a request for the person's name or job title. They will say no if they are unhappy, but most people are delighted to appear in the papers.

Other practical tips on interviewing are found in my book, *JournoLISTS: 201 Ways to Improve Your Journalism* (Ituri).

Keep your notes and recordings. Every interview does, or should, leave a deposit of notes or recordings. Even if we've conducted an impromptu interview and have had to keep it in our head, it's essential for later accuracy to make notes as soon as we can.

Both journalistically and legally, these notes and recordings may be called up. If there is a "comeback" about an article from a source or a reader, the record will be vital in substantiating the accuracy of what we wrote.

In the event of a libel action or some other legal complaint, the notebook or recording may be central to our defence. Written notes are better in a notebook than on scraps of paper. The evidence of loose sheets of paper can easily be faked by being written up later. A reporter's notebook with the stories appearing in date order has more credibility because it's less likely to have been faked.

Editorial comebacks usually are known within a few days, although there are no guarantees. A foreign resident, for example, may receive the publication two or three weeks late, and only then decide to complain.

Libel cases must be started within one year from the publishing date apart from "exceptional circumstances". That's a nasty get-out, so it's safer to keep notes and records for six years (the general time limit for civil actions). It's tedious but necessary.

Lawyers love documents and pictures as hard evidence. We may choose to keep the records longer for our own sake. Perhaps years later we may decide to write a book about a subject where those old notes will be valuable again.

Build in a safety margin before the deadline. Meeting our deadlines isn't merely a matter of honour, it's a necessity for the freelance who wants to keep working. The journalist with a reputation for missing deadlines is as unattractive to an employer as an actor who is late on set.

For the feature writer this means careful scheduling. News events can usually be timed quite precisely; no such certainty is possible with features. If our deadline is on Wednesday morning, we can confidently agree to cover an event on Tuesday afternoon. We know when the event will be and (having been given a word limit) how long we can expect to take to write it up. Very little leeway is needed in relation to the deadline.

We can't sensibly say we'll put Tuesday aside to work on a researched feature for Wednesday. We need to start much further back than that, probably several days before. If the subject is highly newsy, the news peg can be updated right on the deadline.

Feature interviews, even by phone, need to be set up. Even if we are on such terms with our sources that we can just phone and speak with them, they may not be in their offices to take our call. It remains astonishing how little time the movers and shakers spend at their desks! We need, in fact, to build in a considerable safety margin before the deadline to give enough time to make contact with the sources we want.

It's desirable to finish features at deadline minus one – a day before the actual deadline. This allows for the feature to stand overnight. A fresh look the next day typically suggests ways of sharpening up the piece. If for some reason this isn't possible, we should let the feature stand for an hour or so, or even a few minutes, before sending it in.

Writers who file a feature immediately after finishing it are being unprofessional.

8 KEEPING EDITORS HAPPY

Writing to length is a good start in pleasing an editor. Writing to length is an old-fashioned virtue that has a disproportionately positive effect on editors. Freelances who get a reputation for overwriting are doing themselves no favours. To underwrite the specified length is almost as bad. The article may be intended to fill a particular spot, and no-one likes a hole in the page.

Hitting the word target has never been easier when computer programs have word counts and we can trim or expand as needed. Gone are the days of manual typewriting when lengths had to be estimated by counting lines and making an assumption about average words per line. Yet editors say it's remarkable how many of today's freelances still don't turn in material to length.

Unless we've arranged in advance to have more words (a request that should be made sparingly), we have to be prepared to sacrifice points, compelling as they may seem at the time. They are apt to seem less compelling later anyway.

What then is meant by "writing to length"? If we've been commissioned for 800 words, it isn't necessary to file 800 words on the nose. The benchmark standard is never to underwrite (for the reason suggested above) and not to overwrite by more than 5% – ie 840 words in this example. In fact, a little "fat" on the article is no bad thing because it allows for tweaks by the subs.

Word counts are for the text alone. We don't include any standfirst (a short description or trailer that stands at or near the top of the article), headline or footnotes that we may submit.

Meeting the deadline is essential. The deadline is sacrosanct in journalism because our article is part of an intricate, time-critical chain of production. We need to distinguish two types of deadline: the submission deadline, which involves us, and the deadline ex-sub-editors, after which the material goes forward to the designers or the printers (depending on the production arrangements).

We shan't be given a submission deadline right on top of the subbing deadline. In the case of features, a fair amount of time may separate the two. This isn't an argument for leeway in meeting our deadline. Among the reasons why not are that the article may have to be seen before pictures are arranged, it may be earmarked for a page to be done at a certain time, or the sub-editor concerned may be in on Wednesday afternoons but not Thursday mornings.

All sorts of excuses are heard for why deadlines are missed: crucial new information emerged at the last minute, we got ill, the baby got ill, our mother-in-law got ill, we suffered a plumbing emergency and so on. In extreme cases we can agree an extension of the deadline with the editor – but this is a card that can be played only rarely if we want to keep working.

In the previous chapter it was suggested not to work right up to the deadline, allowing ourselves time to look at the article afresh later. (News is another matter: the event may fall on the deadline.) Another reason to complete the feature with time in hand before the deadline is to allow for personal or household emergencies.

Clean copy ticks the right box. Overwhelmingly, copy is submitted by email. We should paste the article onto the email itself unless we are told otherwise. Many publications won't open attachments because of the added risk of viruses.

An aspect of clean copy is that it's unambiguously clear what it is and who it's from. At the head of the article we can put in a single line: our name, the date of filing, the length of the text and a single word identifier known as a catchline. A word like DISPUTES invites confusion with other material with the same name. More specific catchlines like AIRLINES or TIDAL hit the right note.

The catchline may be used to locate the article as it moves through the production process. It isn't any sort of headline and, in fact, it's normally better for writers not to offer headlines. This is the province of the subs, who know the likely space available.

We can feel free to offer standfirsts or footnotes (citing the writer's special experience or mentioning her book, for example), but we have no obligation to do so. The commissioned length of the article refers to the text alone.

Good, clean copy is free of factual and legal errors (see below), and is also tidy in the smaller but still consequential areas. It's free of grammatical errors, hence the need if we're weak in that area to brush it up. Copy is also free of spelling mistakes. Spellcheckers in computer programs help but can't pick out properly spelt words used in the wrong context – *affect* and *effect*, for example.

Regular contributors should make an effort to absorb house presentation style. From a cosmic perspective, it matters not at all if the date is written as *25 December* or *December 25*, or that percentages are written as words (*per cent*) or a symbol (%). Newspapers and magazines like to be consistent, however. If we regularly write things the wrong way, we are proclaiming that we take no interest in how our article came out in print.

And if we insist on writing *Mr.*, *Mrs.* and *Dr.* we are declaring our ignorance not of house style but of the 21st century. Those points are long dead and buried!

Editors need to rely on our accuracy. Experienced editors and sub-editors develop a "nose" for factual errors in copy. However, this mainly concerns matters of general knowledge like dates in history or past events. No editor can know that we have quoted someone correctly from our interview, or given the right figures from previously unpublished information.

Sub-editors used to be called a newspaper's *last line of defence* against errors. Unfortunately, for various reasons – which include not enough staff, leakage of experienced workers to more lucrative occupations and a preoccupation with the technical aspects of copy fitting and page makeup – checking standards aren't what they were.

More than ever, we are on our own in ensuring the accuracy of the content.

Interview quotes should be constructed from our notebook or from a recording, not from memory. The *rule of two* should apply to any but the most obvious facts, or information attributed to a reliable source. This means that the point is stood up by two independent sources – a website and an informant, for example. Two websites may be enough, but information is often copied from one site to the next to the next and so on. A mistake in the prime source is therefore perpetuated.

One of my worst mistakes was to urge readers to visit a mansion that had burnt to the ground 10 years previously. I took the information from an out-of-date book without substantiating it. This was many years ago. It was the sort of lesson that, once learnt, never needs to be repeated.

Some mistakes have legal consequences. To say that a firm has stopped trading whereas it's trading from another location will cost that firm business. The newspaper or magazine may have to make an unpublicised financial settlement. Even mistakes that don't cost money mean embarrassing printed apologies or readers' letters.

As freelances, we can't afford to be seen as error-prone. Our aim must be for our work not to feature in an apology paragraph or to be called into question by readers.

Know your law. To say that a person was dismissed from his previous firm when he wasn't will very likely cost the newspaper or magazine a grovelling apology plus a financial settlement. The statement damages the man's future job prospects and reflects on his character.

So clearly we need to know something about the law as it affects the news media. Just as importantly, we need to know where to look for information about the law. The bible is *McNae's Essential Law for Journalists*, which is updated every two years or so to keep pace with this changing field. It's a book that should be on every freelance's shelf.

The fundamentals of the law tend not to change, however. The two most important areas for working freelances are *libel* and *copyright*. The latter is covered in Chapter 10, Copyright Issues. The example at the start of this section is an example of libel.

The best short definition of libel is *A false statement about someone to his or her discredit*. It's crucial to realise that the law doesn't prevent us saying rude things – so long as they are true. If they aren't, the offended party can sue for damages and costs.

In practice, we shouldn't be frightened but we should be careful. If what we are planning to report is likely to damage someone or some organisation in their finances or their reputation, we need to be sure we can prove the statements if called upon. One of the difficulties of libel is that the onus of proof is on the defence.

One of the trickiest areas is called *innuendo*. A hidden or extended meaning is just as libellous as a plain, false statement. There's nothing particularly hidden about saying *The vicar likes a drink or three*. We might as well just say he's an alcoholic. Other cases of innuendo are subtler; thus it's easy to make a libellous statement without meaning to.

I once wrote (in what was intended as a friendly short item) that a Yorkshire landowner *lived mainly in London and only rarely visited his estate*. This was held by the newspaper's – perhaps over-cautious – lawyer to imply absentee landlordism, a defamatory concept. Rather than risk losing the case, the newspaper paid up!

A colourful intro is a plus in a feature article. The structures of feature articles and news reports are radically different. The ideal news report has the shape called an *inverted pyramid*, in which the first paragraph describes the main, specific point of the event. Other information is given in descending order of importance, with the final par (paragraph) least important of all.

Features, being about issues rather than events, typically begin in a more discursive way with the theme introduced some way into the piece. It's usually a mistake to start the feature too baldly, ie stating in the first par what it's all about. The aim is to whet readers' appetites to prepare them for the long haul of many hundreds of words.

Feature intros may be several pars long. The types include:
- Mood intro, painting a word picture of the scene.
- Case-in-point intro, focusing on an incident or situation that typifies the issue we are writing about.
- Quotation intro – a direct quote that dramatically illustrates the theme.
- Question into – an apt question that intrigues us into the subject matter.

A typical case-in-point intro was written by Danny Lee in the *Guardian*, heading up an article on the dangers of drivers becoming distracted. It begins:

"Stefan Jones was driving to work along an A road just outside Birmingham with his wife Fiona in the front seat when the radio started to play up. It was not the first time and Stefan reached across to the passenger side to adjust it as he always did…"

Where is this going? Three sentences later, we learn that Stefan's fiddling with the radio caused a head-on collision, "killing him and leaving his wife a widow. Stefan was 25."

This is a more interesting way of getting into the subject than ploddingly declaring that in-car distractions are a major cause of road accidents.

The extended nature of many intros is a reason why features are said to consist of three parts: beginning, middle and end. In fact, if we are stuck for an intro, we can try writing the middle first. An intro idea is likely to emerge as we write.

Endings are vital for features. A strong ending is a key difference between features and news. Unfortunately, writers who take a huge amount of trouble over their intros too often neglect their "outros".

Types of outro include a firm conclusion, a tasty quote, a thought-provoking question, even a joke that sums the whole thing up.

My prize for the neatest outro would probably go to Giles Coren for his interview with Umberto Eco, published in the *Times*. Throughout the article Coren made clear that the polymathic Italian author is so stupendously clever that mortals can't cope. The last par reads:

> *Relieved at my imminent departure, he popped another cigarette into his mouth. It was the wrong way round, filter outermost, and for an instant, a couple of never-to-be-repeated seconds before he turned it round, I knew something Umberto Eco didn't.*

Notice that Coren's writing is confident enough to let this telling little vignette run; also that the final six words punch home the message.

Three to five quoted sources are needed for a news-related feature. One of the biggest markets is for news-related features – informative articles on issues of topical interest. These articles combine facts with interpretation, with little place for our own opinions. The focus is on the sources.

Editors are keen for such features to be properly substantiated. The ideal number of persons to be quoted is between three to five. If all five are named, so much the better. Inevitably, however, situations arise where some sources can't be named. They should still be identified – "a surgeon at a teaching hospital", "a leading London solicitor" and so on.

An article consisting entirely of "ghost sources" like these is unlikely to appeal to an editor; some at least of the sources need to be named.

Features can be over-sourced as well as under-sourced. To cram seven or eight quoted individuals into an article isn't a sign of impressive research. It over-eggs the pudding, leaving readers confused or unclear about what is the message of the feature.

The idea of three to five sources applies almost regardless of the length of the article. It's a matter of structure. Thus it applies to an article of 2,000 words as much as one of 800 words. Above 2,000 words is another story, but very few articles in newspapers and magazines pass that limit.

Sub-editing experience helps to improve writing. A freelance writer who does sub-editing shifts as a bread-and-butter staple (described in Chapter 1) has the bonus of becoming a better writer. It's impossible for someone with subbing experience to waffle with the same joyous abandon as before.

Waffly writing shouldn't be confused with colour writing, examples of which were quoted earlier in this chapter. Waffle (also known as gobbledegook) expresses ideas at length for no gain: *adverse weather conditions* is simply *bad weather*; *in spite of the fact that* is a long-winded way of saying *although*; *seating accommodation* means nothing more than *seats*; *in short supply* seems innocuous but it doesn't earn its passage as *scarce* does.

Sub-editors dislike long, rambling sentences and know the impact of breaking them into two. A useful idea is to look hard at any sentence which has more than two structural elements – for example, a relative clause introduced by *which* and a second statement following the conjunction *and*:

The Battle of Hastings, which was fought in 1066, was a turning point in English history, and added a new tier of overlords.

This becomes

> The Battle of Hastings, which was fought in 1066, was a turning point in English history. It added a new tier of overlords.

or

> The Battle of Hastings was fought in 1066. It was a turning point in English history, and added a new tier of overlords.

Everybody will easily find other sorts of sentences with more than two structural elements. Here's another example:

> Even though it may not always seem so/ shares tend to outperform bonds/ although shares should be invested for the medium to long term.

Shorter sentences are one of the main yardsticks of readability. The other is the amount of long words – broadly, those of three or more syllables. We neither can nor should *eliminate/get rid of* all long words, but words that add nothing to the shorter alternative should be chopped. In the previous sentence, *eliminate* and *get rid of* mean the same. By using the three short words instead of the one long one, we express ourselves more clearly.

There are hundreds of such words and phrases in English. Sometimes it's one short word for one long one: *facilitate* means *help*; *initiate* means *start*.

Once we start thinking in these terms, editors will be delighted at our new, tight writing.

RUNNING A BUSINESS

Expenses are deducted from fee income to give pre-tax profit. The freelance's equivalent of a salary is net pre-tax profit – what is left after business expenses are deducted. We receive fees gross, with income tax due twice a year, in January and July.

This arrangement is helpful because we have the use of all the money for a time. The arrangement is so helpful to the self-employed that HM Revenue and Customs has over the years forced many types of workers onto pay-as-you-earn (PAYE). They include casual sub-editors and reporters. If we do shifts, we'll most likely be paid net (with income tax and national insurance deducted). This is a second income stream, and is declared separately from fee income.

As freelances, we can charge against income a wide range of operating expenses. These are subtracted from fee income to reach the amount on which tax is charged. Expenses include:

- Train, bus and taxi fares to assignments
- Air travel and associated costs of overseas assignments
- Meals and hotel accommodation for assignments
- Purchase (share of cost) of motor car
- Running costs of motor car for assignments

- Business phone calls
- Purchase of computers and other IT equipment
- Internet service provider subscription
- Postage
- Essential newspapers and magazines
- Reference books
- Essential internet access charges
- Advertising and marketing, including website costs
- Secretarial/administrative help
- Training courses
- Accountancy fees
- Office rent, rates and utilities OR share of home utilities
- Office furniture
- Business bank account charges
- Petty cash

None of these is an allowance. We have actually to spend the money to claim it. We also need to be able to prove it if necessary through receipts and so on. *Even if our expenses are reimbursed, we still show them as outgoings* (if we didn't, this would say we made more profit from the assignment than we did).

Many of the items on the expenses side of the accounts are to be charged *proportionally*. We can't, for instance, charge the whole cost of buying and running a car when mostly it's for our private use.

Freelances (unless they are operating as a limited company – see below) with an annual income of less than £15,000 can take advantage of a simpler procedure with their tax return.

They don't have to show expenses in categories, but just list the total.

Keep a cash book or the electronic equivalent to show income and outgoings. The key business record for the self-employed is the cash book, or its electronic equivalent. This should be arranged in monthly sections, showing all income and outgoings.

Traditionally, income is listed on right-hand pages and outgoings on left-hand pages. If we have registered for value-added tax, the book will show VAT amounts for each entry where applicable alongside the full amounts paid or received.

Receipts and payments need to be supported with documents. A byproduct of computerisation is that businesses end up with a mixture of paper and electronic records. Yet it's best to have all records under one roof. I find it easier to keep records on paper, printing out as necessary. Some others may prefer to keep all records electronically, scanning in as required. (The paper originals of some legal documents need to be kept, however.)

One of the benefits of monthly accounting is that we can easily see where we stand as the year proceeds. The year's running totals are the most reliable indicator. Freelance income typically fluctuates. A single month's result may suggest triumph or disaster, while over the year reality may be somewhere in the middle.

It's highly desirable to have a separate bank account for our freelance activities. Our accountant if we have one – or a tax inspector examining our affairs – will wish to carry out a bank reconciliation. This involves matching cash book entries with entries on the bank statements.

Unless we have formed a limited company, we should use a second personal account rather than a business current account. The charges on business accounts are better avoided if we can; by contrast, personal accounts may pay *us* interest, or at the least charge us less.

Charge to expenses only what we know we can defend. The freelance working from home incurs expenses that are partly business and partly private. These include the common use of the telephone and the home office's share of household utilities. There may be a motor car somewhere that isn't used for private as well as business trips, but the tax inspector won't believe it!

In other words, although we use the phone and the car for business, and we burn heat and light in our home-office, we can't charge all the phone, gas, electric and car bills to the business. The amounts claimed must be proportional to the business use.

With phone bills, a claim of a half or two-thirds for business wouldn't be seen as surprising; seven-eighths for business would be. A fifth or even a quarter of heat, light and water bills, depending on the size of the home, would be reasonable. The cost of car purchase may be split between business and private. Mileage rates as calculated by the motoring organisations include the overheads of car ownership as well as the cost of fuel. Therefore, if we charge mileage for business trips, we can't also charge for road tax, maintenance and depreciation.

We can properly charge in full the purchase of a computer, the cost of newspapers in reasonable quantities, a subscription to an internet portal and accountancy fees. These items certainly have private value – I shall certainly book my holiday online even though the computer was acquired for business – but we'd be unlucky to be challenged. It's open to us to argue that, apart from business needs, we could do without these items.

The golden rule is to charge only what we know we can defend, erring on the side of caution. Once the Revenue suspect us of over-claiming, they can take us apart. They will demand chapter and verse for our outgoings and the reason for them.

Keep business records long-term. We may be untroubled by the tax authorities for years. We may never hear from them. What may draw attention to ourselves is an item that differs greatly from the freelance norm. Travel and accommodation is an example. Heaven help us if this category is swollen by the cost of private trips loaded onto the business!

We may not hear from the Revenue for years, but then... If they inspect us, officials may want to go back a very long time – and we need the business records in order to defend ourselves. Without them, it may be impossible to remember why we met So-and-so for lunch five years ago. Even if we remember, where's the proof that we ate the lunch that we have charged for?

The benchmark is to keep all business records for seven years.

Records mean cash books, bank statements (but not cheque stubs and pay-in books), receipts, bills and payment notifications, and diaries. This last may clarify whom we met, and why. Even our cuttings books – which we keep for other reasons – may prove the legitimacy of a disputed item by showing what came of the meeting.

The need to keep business records for so long raises two issues: storage and back-up. If the records are paper-based, anyone who doesn't have a loft may have a storage problem. If the records are electronic, we need to ensure that everything – everything – is backed up. It was suggested earlier that we should avoid a hybrid system where some records are on paper and others are electronic.

Keep track of payments due. One of the biggest bugbears in freelancing is the late-paying client. There are lots of them. The newspaper or magazine that pays within the customary 30 days seems to be in a minority of clients, big or small. Two or three months after publication is commonplace.

It's essential to keep track of fees due, and to be prepared to chase late payments. Companies typically have payment runs at a certain time of the week or month, so some variation in the speed of settlement is inevitable. If a client regularly pays within 60 days, we may decide to live with this. Payments after more than two months aren't acceptable in any way; we should press for a speedier outcome.

Freelances have often been caught by the collapse of smaller media companies with no hope of seeing their money

– another reason for not letting an unpaid debt drift on.

Since 1998, we have had the law on our side in the form of the Late Payment of Commercial Debts (Interest) Act. This allows creditors to charge interest, at a specified level, on debts unpaid after 30 days. Freelances have proved reluctant to use the act because they fear editors will hold it against them. The fear is probably exaggerated, but in any case the act is a doomsday weapon only to be used when other approaches have failed.

The first step, after 30 days, is politely to remind the commissioning editor that the payment is overdue. He or she will pass this message to the accounts department. If this doesn't produce a result, we go directly to accounts. An experienced freelance, Judy Yorke, has found that soft talk unlocks more doors. She told the union newsletter *BAJ News*: "I speak sweetly to the accounts department and ask them to chase it up for me."

The simplest and most effective way of keeping track of payments is a diary or wallchart. The diary can be paper or electronic.

We enter in the diary each article under the date when it was filed. The single-word identifier (catchline) is the same as that used for the story file. When the payment has been made we tick it off in the diary. The procedure is the same with the wallchart.

Both systems let us see at a glance whether payments are up to date.

Expect to spend 10% of work time on admin. No-one ever went into journalism because of its administrative prospects. However, as freelances we are running a business as well as engaging in creative activity. This means spending a certain amount of time on admin – not only keeping the finances straight but also marketing ourselves professionally. Cultivating contacts and having a website are ways of maintaining our profile (see below).

Being up to date with admin saves us time in the long run. We avoid, for example, the last-minute scramble for documents and general chaos when the annual accounts are due. A benchmark figure for admin in an established freelance business is 10% – the equivalent of a half-day in a five-day week.

Fortunately, there are facilities to help us save time. Newspapers and some magazines generate payments without receiving invoices. This system, called *self-billing*, spares us a clerical chore.

An accountant or book-keeper is worth the few hundred pounds it costs to avoid the time-consuming morass of the annual tax return. Their fee is a deductible business expense. It comes even cheaper if we ask HM Revenue and Customs to work out the tax for us: they do it free.

Think marketing. A personal website is the freelance's main marketing tool. This should include biodata, an indication of subjects that we cover, contact information and any testimonials or tributes we can grab hold of. Its main value is as an archive of our published articles. Note that unless we have the copyright in these articles we may need permission to republish them. The law applies even to personal websites, although it's unlikely that an editor would be too bothered. Copyright is explained in the next chapter.

The archive builds up our professional credibility. Editors as well as potential public relations clients may like to refer to it, where they can get a feel for our work. It's worth the modest investment to have our own domain: **www.pulfordmedia.co.uk** is more persuasive than **www.pulfordmedia.webhost.co.uk** because it implies a more substantial operation.

Editors need individual pitches but, for others, mailshots or e-shots may be appropriate. These include local businesses that we are targeting for public relations or proof-reading work. Unless they draw a response, these speculative shots should be followed with a phone call in a week or so. They should also prominently feature a reference or a link to the website.

Another form of marketing involves keeping in touch with our contacts. This is an investment for the future. Because we have kept up the connection, people will be more willing to talk to us when we need to. A polite – and practical – touch that is always appreciated is to send a cutting or photocopy of the published article in which the source is quoted. Include a short note to thank them again for their help. This shows we don't take them for granted, which sadly many journalists do.

Once upon a time, famous writers prided themselves on answering their letters. Perhaps most still do. I received when a schoolboy an individually worded and personally signed letter from P.G. Wodehouse, one of the most famous writers on the planet. Many journalists seem to feel free to ignore letters and emails. Unless they are crank or abusive messages, we should respond to all our personal correspondence. It's not only common politeness but also good marketing.

Think about registering for value added tax below the compulsory threshold. A substantial income is needed before we must register for value-added tax, or VAT. The threshold is regularly raised. In 2008 it was £67,000 of gross annual income. However, we can voluntarily sign up with a lower income.

VAT-registered journalists add 15% tax to fees. (This reduction from the standard 17.5% level was introduced in late-2008, when it was described as temporary.) The big benefit is that we can offset the VAT on business purchases, paying the government the difference between what we have collected on our *supplies* (*output tax*) and what we are reclaiming (*input tax*).

This means that we keep a chunk of the VAT we've collected – in other words, getting items like computer and office equipment, stationery, hotel accommodation and meals free of the tax the public must pay.

HM Revenue and Customs say there is no lower limit of earnings for voluntary registration. What matters is that the activity is a *bona fide business* (even if carried on by an individual) seeking to make a profit, and that it's *ongoing* (not a one-off job). They put it this way:

"Generally business is seen as a continuing activity carried on with the intention of making supplies for a consideration. Non-business activities can include those carried on as a hobby or supplies made in a purely private capacity (for example the sale of personal belongings)."

VAT can be a book-keeping headache for some businesses, but for freelance journalists outputs (fees) and inputs (expenses) are likely to be relatively few each month. It's in most freelances' interest, even those at a modest level of earnings, to apply for registration.

For businesses with an annual turnover of less than £150,000 (almost every journalist in the country!), Revenue and Customs offer a simple arrangement called the flat rate scheme. This involves collecting VAT at the appropriate level and handing over *a lesser percentage* of the gross amount. This sounds as likely as a perpetual motion machine, but there is no catch. We can't reclaim input VAT, though, which may erode the benefit of the flat rate scheme.

We need to ask our accountant or other financial adviser before signing up, but the flat rate scheme will save us money *provided income substantially exceeds vattable expenses*. This is usually the case with a freelance journalist.

A limited company may be worthwhile when income is large. Self-employed people customarily trade as a limited company when income becomes large. This is because of the tax advantages.

The accounting obligations, however, make the decision to incorporate trickier than to decide to register for VAT.

These include the need annually to make two separate returns to Companies House and to publish accounts – a job that best involves an accountant. Much of this information goes onto the open, public record.

There is also the need to operate a payroll, even if we are the only staff member. Monthly payments of tax and national insurance have to be made to HMRC, as do monthly and annual returns. An annual corporation tax return must also be made.

The cash book needs to be properly kept so that income and expenditure items can be reconciled with the matching entries in the bank statements. It requires a separate business bank account, costing more to operate than a personal account.

We'll also find ourselves involved with two sets of tax returns – for the company and for ourselves.

None of these activities is insuperably difficult even for the solo worker, but they suggest why forming a company is usually left until income has grown. In recent years an annual profit of £30,000 has commonly been suggested.

A limited company gives us an extra layer of credibility. Financially, it becomes attractive at a certain level because we can take part of our income as a dividend on our shareholding. Dividends are taxed at a lower rate than salaries – in 2009 10% compared with the income tax basic rate of 20%.

Imagine that on a turnover of £50,000 we make a profit of £30,000. We'll pay less tax if we take £20,000 as salary and £10,000 as dividend than if we take all £30,000 as salary.

The salary has to be realistic. To take £1,000 as salary and

£29,000 as dividend is too obviously a device to avoid tax. People who use this tactic – a common saloon bar boast – are running the risk of being hanged, drawn and quartered by the tax authorities.

10 COPYRIGHT ISSUES

Know how press syndication works. The essence of syndication is sharing material. Major British newspapers over many years have evolved systems to sell their material to other publications. Most of these are overseas, in which case articles and pictures may be available for publication at the same time as the originating newspaper.

Within Britain, because of competition considerations, the material may be used by others only after first publication.

Many journalists have heard about press syndication in the United States. There, where regionally based media remain dominant, words, pictures and cartoons are issued simultaneously to scores or even hundreds of outlets. Most of us in Britain remain unaware of the equally elaborate arrangements on our own doorsteps. For freelances it pays to know because it's our material that is being syndicated!

Selected material may be sent to subscribing clients by email; alternatively (or in addition), subscribers may have *lifting rights*. This means they take whatever content they please from the newspaper or web edition. A further aspect of syndication is *spot sales*: non-subscribers may from time to time buy particular articles or pictures.

Traditionally, features were the staple of syndication. Email and the internet, by delivering content faster, have made the syndication of news more practicable.

The operation of a syndication service is similar, on a vastly smaller scale, to that of a news agency like Reuter or Associated Press. From the newspaper's point of view, it's a useful way of offsetting some of the costs of editorial content. No-one makes a fortune from words; pictures command better prices.

Commercial databases are another way in which our material may be used. These are archives that the mainly corporate customers access for a fee.

To make extended use of freelance content, publications need to have the necessary rights. Commissioning letters will be worded accordingly. Only very powerful freelances – or freelances with very powerful material – can limit these rights, leaving themselves with more opportunities for re-selling (see below).

Knowing copyright law pays dividends. Copyright is a law of intellectual property, protecting among others articles, photographs and drawings. It doesn't have to be asserted: it's inherent in the piece of work, with or without the international symbol ©.

Work by employees done as part of their duties is owned by the employer. As freelances, however, we keep the copyright in an article unless we have given it up. Strictly speaking, this assignment needs to be in writing but not every publication works that way.

Some ask the freelance to sign a waiver with the commissioning letter. Others simply assert what rights they are buying. This could be challenged in law, although it could be argued that accepting a commissioning letter, especially repeatedly, is an assignment of the copyright.

If there is no commissioning letter with a copyright clause, all we have sold are the first British serial rights – ie the client has first use of the material in a periodical within the United Kingdom. We are free to sell outside the country and for second use in the UK. In the real world, we should try to find out about the client's syndication arrangements, if any.

A friend who was a financial journalist sold a feature to a technical magazine in Chicago, believing he had the overseas rights. At the same time, a British newspaper syndicated the same feature to the US editor's deadly rival. The result was two angry editors in Chicago, another one in London and a correspondent on the back foot.

We need to avoid this sort of fiasco. On the other hand, a client may have no syndication arrangements and if we don't offer the article to others we shall have missed selling opportunities. Many freelances don't make the best financial use of their material. This is through ignorance of copyright and syndication.

A commissioning letter should state the rights being acquired. The copyright "cake" can be apportioned in many ways, from the thin slice of first British serial rights to no slices at all in the form of the copyright in its entirety. It's not a black and white matter of selling the copyright or not selling it. For instance, we might retain all serial rights outside the United Kingdom; or dispose of serial rights worldwide but retain the rights to spin-off uses like book publication.

First British serial rights means that the item can't be syndicated or used again in the original publication without further permission from the writer or photographer. Many a photographer has been able to demand a further fee for repeat use.

Any publication with syndication arrangements should sensibly set out in the commissioning letter the rights being acquired. Some don't. In that situation it's in our interest to ask for the matter to be clarified.

Refinements of copyright law include first and further uses, and exclusive and non-exclusive uses. A *Guardian* standard contract specified exclusive, worldwide syndication rights for three months, followed by non-exclusive rights for the period of the copyright. This allowed the contributor to re-sell his or her work after three months – albeit with approval to ensure no conflict with the newspaper's own syndication.

The paper was certainly giving itself enough time to carry on syndicating. Copyright lasts for 70 years from the author's death. In the case of a 25-year-old, the period of the copyright might well be 130 years from the date of publication!

This is a long time to surrender rights, although still superior to giving up the copyright. Regretfully, in a growingly complex digital environment many clients simply swallow the whole cake.

Some newspapers and magazines share with the freelance the proceeds of 'selling on' an article. Newspapers and magazines may distinguish between their regular syndication service and spot sales. Using an article in the daily syndication service is included in the fee. Spot sales are another matter.

Britain's middle and mass market newspapers not infrequently approach the upmarket papers to reprint features, generating a spot sale. Another type of spot sale occurs when the original publisher approaches a publication that doesn't subscribe to the regular syndication service to offer a particular article.

A dramatic example of spot selling occurred until relatively recently with an upmarket newspaper that sold features to a tabloid for re-use. Under the then syndication terms, freelance writers received no extra fee. The tabloid actually paid more to reprint the articles than the original fees to the writers – so the first paper got the articles for nothing, and made a profit. This situation was clearly unfair. In a negotiation involving the National Union of Journalists, it was abolished in favour of a profit split.

In this case and others, freelances share in the fruits of spot sales. The *Guardian* standard contract mentioned in the previous section provided for the proceeds to be split 50:50 between the newspaper and the writer.

Arrangements for spot sales should be included in the commissioning letter or any document that may accompany it. If necessary, we should ask for this to be written in. Complex matters of syndication and copyright aren't suitable to be left for informal understandings or spoken promises.

Some freelances fear they will mark their card if they demand to know about copyright and syndication details. This fear is unnecessary: we are more likely to be respected for being professional than blamed for being awkward. However, as mentioned at the start of the book, the first concern of beginning freelances is to be published. Any negotiations over copyright and syndication are usually better left until we are more established.

We can re-sell articles ourselves – provided we have the rights. An active syndication department producing spot sales is to be thoroughly welcomed. This is extra profit for us for no extra work. Too often, however, the complaint from freelances is that not enough is done to sell the material.

There is lots we can do for ourselves, provided we have the relevant rights. It may be that second serial rights are non-exclusive, allowing both us and the commissioning newspaper to sell them. But if we have given up the copyright there is nothing we can do except alert the syndication department to any selling prospects we hear about.

Other newspapers or magazines within the UK are potential sources of re-publication. These can be rich seams. Trade, technical and professional magazines may find some sorts of general feature suitable for their readerships. Britain's regional dailies have little overlap in circulations, permitting us to sell to several at once "exclusively within your circulation area". (Where circulation areas do overlap, with the *Yorkshire Post* and the *Northern Echo*, for example, we should sell to one or the other, not both.)

None of these publications will be remotely concerned that the article has appeared in a national newspaper. Specialist magazines and regional newspapers know their readers take a range of national papers. Thus the reader overlap with any individual national is of no consequence.

Fees for second use in specialist and regional media will be small. (Actually, the fees aren't great in these sectors for original articles!) Remember, however, that this is extra profit for no extra work beyond that of pitching the offer. We should resist any request to amend or adjust the material for re-publication. To do that means more work without the benefit of an appropriate fee for a fresh article.

The first time we pitch to a newspaper or magazine with an article to reprint we should do so by telephone. On later occasions, when we know them, email is fine.

Commercial syndication agencies offer to place the material for us. They aren't widely used by writing freelances because of limited results. The market for words is weak. Even major newspapers find this, offering their syndication services at knock-down rates. Commercial agencies are better prospects for photos and cartoons, where the market is far stronger.

Foreign publications are promising sources of re-publication. As long as we have rights clearance, newspapers and magazines around the world are good potential outlets to re-use an article. The approach need not be limited to English-language media. The world has a big appetite for material from Britain, particularly if it's offbeat or quirky.

The difficulty is to make contact with these media. We can find the names of major publications in the Benn's or Willings media directories, but what then? Reaching the right person abroad can be tough. Telephoning is probably not worth the time and trouble, even if we use Skype or other VOIP (voice over internet protocol) systems at negligible cost. Email is likely to be more productive.

We don't need to wait to be asked before sending the article itself. We can send it speculatively, saying the article is available at the user's standard rate. Point out in a covering message that the piece hasn't been sponsored or paid for by any company or organisation. It will have a greater chance of acceptance if it's recognised as editorial, not public relations advertorial.

Emailing not phoning, and sending the whole article not an outline, are the opposites of what we should do within our country!

Having filed the article, wait to see what comes back. Remember to paste the article into the email as well as sending it as an attachment. Potential users may be unwilling to open an attachment from an unknown sender.

Remember to include bank account details including IBAN and Swiftcode information. The client is more likely to use these electronic payment systems than to issue a cheque. It's an honour system that will almost always work with reputable clients. If after a number of articles we've had no bites, we can stop sending.

We need to make clear the rights status of the article. If the original publisher has syndicated the article in a particular country, our offer is non-exclusive. If it hasn't been syndicated, we can offer it exclusively within the country.

Syndication clients of major British newspapers frequently have their own syndication clients, at home and abroad. We may need to ban dissemination outside the recipient's country (in case it clashes with our own distribution). However, the fewer restrictions we put on an article the greater its chances of being used.

Send to multiple outlets where circulations don't overlap. We maximise potential sales if we send an article to many outlets at once, provided their circulation areas don't overlap. Why send to one or two countries when, at zero extra cost thanks to email, we can send to 20 or 30? We need to specify that users can't sell on the material internationally; otherwise it may end up in a country we have also sent to!

The same approach applies to regionally based newspapers within a country, so long as they don't have substantial circulation overlaps.

Michael Cope, a Canadian-based journalist, wrote a weekly newsletter. He sent it speculatively to newspapers all over the southern neighbour, the United States. Because American newspapers were, and are, mainly local, he was profitably selling the same article many times over.

Michael mailshotted his target newspapers for up to a year. He told me that he was usually ignored for a long time. Then a single article would creep in. Then another. The gap between published articles gradually lessened until in many cases he was a regular columnist on that paper's op-ed page.

Michael never priced his articles. He told editors to pay at their standard rate. It was an honour system, and it worked.

The moral is to keep sending for a considerable time. It's no use expecting our work, brilliant as it is, to sail in the first time, or even the second and third times.

Haydn Emery, my colleague in running journalism training courses, developed an ingenious service of advertorial features that he distributed to regional newspapers around Britain. The beauty of his system was that articles were tied to the season – what to do in the garden in spring, what to look for in a boiler now winter is coming on, and so on. Just as the seasons come round, so did Haydn's articles. With a little tweaking each year, the articles were as good as new.

That's a lesson for us all in using material to the full.

As well as being re-sold, material may be re-worked into further articles. Copyright adheres in the words, not the facts, the ideas or the angles. If we significantly alter the words, we create a new article. A new copyright comes into existence, and the article isn't subject to restrictions on further use.

This may be more promising than re-selling the original article as a way of extracting the most benefit from the material. In practical terms, it's not enough to tinker with the phraseology. No editor will feel that this is a genuinely new article.

What then must we do to generate new articles from the same body of information?

* The central idea, or theme, can be the same. A medieval church has been safeguarded for future generations despite being stranded in a military firing area (Imber on Salisbury Plain). Consumers are failing to benefit from health supplements because they won't pay for premium products. And so on.

* Core facts can be the same but each article has different additional facts.
* The named sources can be the same but with substantial differences in the quotes.
* The intro and outro – which give much of the flavour to an article – are distinctively different.

The ensuing articles will be sufficiently separate. Even so, our target publications need space between them. It wouldn't be wise to try to sell such articles concurrently to competing clients.

Copyright is a negotiable situation. For most freelances, keeping the rights to syndicate their own work is a dream. Newspapers and magazines tend to demand rights on a take-it-or-leave it basis. At several places in this book, it has been pointed out that copyright belongs to the freelance unless he or she agrees to part with it. Here is the place to examine the point.

We should convince ourselves that copyright is a negotiable situation. Sometimes. We can expect to negotiate an improvement on a publication's standard rights terms if (a) we are very important – ie our byline is seen as highly recognisable to readers – or (b) the material we offer is unusually strong.

When I worked for the *Guardian* syndication service, almost all regular contributors, even well known ones, were on standard terms. A handful, including John Pilger and Julie Burchill, had special arrangements. We had to memorise the names so that their articles didn't slip into the service by mistake. In some cases, we couldn't distribute in particular countries, especially the United States. In other cases, we couldn't syndicate at all.

Such restrictions help writers, who scoop 100% of the proceeds of further sales. Publications wouldn't be left with a syndication service if special arrangements became widespread, so they will resist where they can.

It may be easier than we think, however. Experienced freelance Judy Yorke shared her experiences on the other side of the table with the union newsletter *BAJ News*. "I used to be a commissioning editor and though we were always told to get all rights where possible I wasn't prepared to lose a story over it," she said.

The moral must be to know our strength and be prepared to use it.

11 BROADENING OUT (TV/RADIO/BOOKS)

Be proactive in looking for radio and TV opportunities. Freelancing for newspapers and magazines is where the greatest opportunities lie. Print is the easiest of the media in which to get started. It's not, however, the best paid. That is television.

Radio, in its multifarious outlets, usually brings adequate rather than brilliant returns. It can also be deeply satisfying with the creative challenge to paint word pictures and to hold the audience through the single sense of hearing.

TV and radio are open to us when we are established. There are those who make their living entirely from these media, and it would be presumptuous to think we can bed-hop at will. Nevertheless, broadcasting values journalistic techniques. On the news and current affairs side it goes out of its way to stress that it's journalism. If we have a name, a distinctive specialism or significant personal experiences, broadcasting will want us.

We must be proactive in seeking out opportunities. It's a mistake to imagine that at a certain stage in our career people will beat a path to our door. Always we have to make our own openings – by networking, by putting up ideas, by leveraging one break into a second and third and so on.

Deploy specialist knowledge on radio and TV. For the experienced freelance writer, radio and television work is a natural way to broaden out. As generalists, we have very little claim on this work. From a commissioning editor's point of view, we don't bring much to the table. It's another matter if we have expertise in a subject of current interest.

One possible route is as a regular contributor to magazine programmes. For example, the writer of a newspaper column about pets was invited to fill a slot in a radio programme on the same subject.

The pay for these activities, particularly in radio, won't be great. On the other hand, they tend to take up not much time – less than writing a newspaper article – and by giving us exposure may lead to more lucrative activities.

A journalistic background is a good credential for radio and TV documentaries. Radio is the easier medium to get into. It's perceived as less glamorous than TV and, more importantly, there is a huge number of outlets nationally, regionally and locally.

Any freelance wanting to work in broadcasting shouldn't turn down the smallest radio station offering the littlest money. It gives us the start of an airtime portfolio. Just as with writers for newspapers and magazines, being broadcast is more important at the beginning than how much we are paid.

Personal experiences are another route into broadcasting. Quarrying our personal experiences is another route into TV and radio. These are more emotional media than print. All journalism recognises the importance of human interest, but from child abuse to Asian tsunamis, ID cards to stealth taxes, broadcast programmes engage our emotions more often and more fully than print can.

A presenter with a connection to the subject matter – a recovering alcoholic on substance abuse, for example – gives added bite to the programme.

That isn't to say that everyone with interesting experiences can become a broadcast journalist. But personal experiences combined with journalism skills and a feel for what is newsy and interesting make a potent combination.

Much programme making is done by independent production companies, some of which are substantial commercial enterprises. Major ones are listed in the *Writers' and Artists' Yearbook*, which is updated annually. The entries show the type of material they are interested in.

We can take heart from the fact that companies list their programme types because they want to hear from us! No surprise there. Ideas are the lifeblood of creative media. In pitching ideas, we should be sure to include the indies along with broadcasters themselves – the channels, networks and stations.

We are part of the message in broadcasting. In print journalism, writers send out messages; in television and radio, reporters and presenters are part of the message. This isn't egotism, although there's plenty of that in broadcasting, but a recognition that audiences react to the sound and appearance of the broadcaster. Rarely will the feelings be analysed. The response is at the gut level of "I like him", "I don't like her",

"I trust her", "I don't trust him".

Our only tool in radio is the voice. We want to sound pleasantly conversational, not too formal, too glib or too strident. The spoken language in an unpressured situation has a natural rise and fall, with our words speeding up and slowing down as we think our way through the sentence we are speaking. It's this naturalness that we want to replicate on air.

We need to be aware in particular that if we are nervous the voice will tend to become a monotone – the opposite of relaxed confidence.

Talking too fast in the sense of gabbling and going on too long are other giveaways for nervousness. But we'll never speak too fast provided we articulate our words clearly. We are more likely to sound too slow because we seem slower to ourselves than we do to others.

The voice is almost as important on television as on radio. Additionally, we have visual features that can make or break us. Dressing wrong will put up a barrier between us and viewers' acceptance. Wearing T-shirt, jeans and trainers on a business programme is as inappropriate as wearing a suit and tie for an outdoor leisure programme!

Leaning forward slightly towards our interviewee shows interest, but too far forward is confrontational. Meanwhile, leaning back in a chair is too casual. Moving hands moderately is natural and good to watch. Flapping or windmilling hands are distracting; pointing and chopping motions are aggressive signals that may win the viewers' support – for the other side.

We should aim for a light, level gaze whether we are looking at an interviewee, a group of people or the camera itself. Poor eye angles give a damaging impression. Eyes towards the ceiling look helpless, towards the floor dejected and sideways avoiding.

Paradoxically, we must study to look and sound natural on air.

Be proactive in looking for opportunities in books. Books are often seen as the pinnacle of a journalist's career. They are contrasted with the ephemera of newspaper and magazine articles. Yet books are only relatively durable. Anyone who doubts it need only consider well known journalist-authors of the recent past who are already forgotten. Who, apart from contemporaries, knows the names of Noel Barber and James Cameron?

A better way to look at books is as an additional activity. The vast majority of authors get more glory than money. Only a handful earn more than £5,000 a year from their books. Yet there is no shortage of people wanting to be writers. Quite the opposite. The book industry grumbles that too many books are published (but continues to produce them), and the "vanity publishing" industry flourishes.

The most effective way to sell most books is for the author to give talks to interested groups, and to have the books for sale afterwards. People like to have autographed copies of work even from unknown writers!

Many of these occasions will be unpaid apart from travel expenses and the sale of the books. However, fees are available for a range of events including conferences, lunchtime talks and after-dinner speaking.

Registering with a speakers' bureau can be a good way to connect with this market. For every politician or national figure who commands many thousands of pounds at a time, there is an army of speakers who are happy with a few hundreds – still useful money for a freelance.

Public speaking, in fact, has emerged as a profession in its own right with a representative body, the Professional Speakers Association. Anyone who wants to take this route should consider getting trained. Many of the presentation issues that were highlighted earlier for TV and radio apply to public speaking.

For the freelance, the reasons to write books are the sense of achievement, the recognition it brings in small or large measure and the professional profile. To be a published author provides a useful springboard into broadcasting (see above).

A publisher is unlikely to hammer on our door because he or she has seen our bylines in a newspaper. As with broadcasting, we must be proactive in seeking out opportunities.

Many books are commissioned because of the authors' work as journalists. It's scarcely an exaggeration to say that every journalist wants to publish a book. Quite a few manage it, and this will, I hope, include readers of this book.

Books are often commissioned or accepted from journalists, who will be in the main writers not sub-editors, specialists not generalists. Journalists appeal to publishers because we are felt to know how to do research and to be safe with facts (at least safer than an "amateur" author!). Avoiding discrediting or libellous mistakes is crucial, and in a 100,000-word manuscript the publisher must take most information on trust.

Specialist writers are more appealing than generalists because they are more likely to get to the bottom of the subject. The publisher is taking the financial risk, and wants to be confident of a return.

Significant or interesting personal experiences may also attract a publisher – just as they may appeal to radio and TV (see above).

If we fail to find a commercial publisher, we may want to consider using a so-called vanity publisher or to publish the book ourselves. The latter will be cheaper, using print-on-demand* technology. Many offerings rejected by commercial publishers aren't bad books; they are simply too specialised to be financially viable.

That goes too for vanity publishing (an unhelpful term) and self-publishing. The difficulty is marketing: we are unlikely to get our money back through sales.

Many journalists have found opportunities in ghost-writing for celebrities who lack the time, inclination and probably the ability to write their books themselves. This job, traditionally seen as unglamorous, has become more attractive in recent years as the ghost has partly materialised. Title pages commonly credit the actual writer (in smaller type) along with the celebrity whose name will sell the book.

---

* A computerised technology without printing plates, allowing short runs or even a single copy of a book to be produced economically.

A book agent isn't essential but it helps. An agent increases our chances of finding a publisher. Both literary agents and publishers are listed in the *Writers' and Artists' Yearbook*, showing the type of material each firm deals with.

More than 100,000 titles are published annually in the UK alone. Supply begets supply, with a mega-pile of manuscripts on offer (fuelled by press articles suggesting that "everyone has a book in them"). Publishers, although they consider direct proposals, depend on agents to do most of the preliminary screening for them.

Even getting onto the books of an established agent nowadays is something of an achievement, never mind finding the publisher! But it's important to try. Agents know the market better than any outsider can. The service will cost us, however. An agent typically takes a commission of 10%-15% (more on overseas sales).

Many of the agents in *Writers' and Artists'* list their submission requirements. If they like the proposal, they will take us on. It's common to require a synopsis plus three sample chapters. So quite an amount of work is needed before we know whether anyone will publish our book.

We mustn't give up if one or two agents or publishers turn us down. Remember Harry Potter, rejected by many publishers until Bloomsbury spotted the potential!

A book is more than an extended article; it's a new area of skill. Writing a book is no harder than writing a feature article on a bigger scale, right? Wrong. The surprise for me when I wrote my first book, *Eating Uganda*, was quite how different the experience was from article writing.

For a start, there was the scale of the project, with even my modest-size (70,000 words) book the length of 70 or so articles. But whereas it would be just a question of time to write 70 articles, this job felt qualitatively different.

Vast amounts of information and quotations disappeared into the chasm of the word count waiting to be filled. Then there is the need to keep a theme going: a book is *about* something (unless it's a collection of essays or a volume of miscellanea). Keeping some sort of thematic unity proved to be the hardest part.

Writers differ in the ways they confront the job. Some erect the scaffolding in detail before they start; others lay the first bricks and watch what happens next. Some start at chapter one and write sequentially to the end; others write in any order that appeals at the time.

It's a pity that the commercial market for pamphlets has vanished. How often do we see a pamphlet for sale in a bookshop? The experience of writing 10,000-20,000 words would be an excellent staging post between articles and books. However, all sorts of organisations, particularly campaigning groups, still produce pamphlets. Distribution may be limited, but they also turn up on websites. We should welcome the chance to write one of these documents.

Local subjects are winners. The story of publishing is littered with rejected manuscripts that went on to become best-selling books. Likewise, remainder bookshops are full of expensively commissioned books that failed to sell. However, one genre finds it hard to fail: local subjects.

History and nostalgia books for villages, towns and counties have become big business about small subjects. Few authors see local books as their life's work, but they are a more predictable market than more ambitious books about national and international subjects.

The publisher can usually count on strong public interest in the local subject. The abundance of photographs and other illustrations in museums, libraries and private collections makes it straightforward to produce visually appealing books. They go on sale in unlikely places – corner shops, post offices, even pubs.

From the writer's point of view, the book will probably have a long shelf life, with a steady sale perhaps for years. This is at a time when authors complain that national publishers frequently dump their books into the remainder shops after only a year.

Local publishers sometimes try to buy all rights to the writer's work for a flat fee (rather than paying a royalty on sales, with the writer keeping the copyright). This is a temptation to be resisted. The traditional advice applies: hang on to your copyrights!

12 AFTERWORD

To be a successful freelance journalist means always to be aware of the news: what is happening and "the topics people are discussing", in the phrase of Lord Northcliffe, founder of the *Daily Mail*.

There is no such thing as a rigid news/feature divide. Far away from the news pages themselves, very little appears in newspapers that doesn't have some sort of topical relevance. Magazines by their nature are less urgent, but the strongest material is still news-related.

Both newspapers and magazines run content that has no connection whatever with news. Some service articles, from beauty tips to car mechanics to crosswords, are entirely timeless. There may be poems and short stories. This material is perfectly good but it isn't journalism.

After specifying *actualities* (events) as the first sort of news, Northcliffe defined news of the second sort as "the 'talking points', the 'features'" [Quoted by Tom Clarke in *My Northcliffe Diary*]. Since Northcliffe's time, in the first part of the 20th century, features have evolved into a separate department of journalism. This shouldn't blind us, however, to the continuing intimate connection with news.

No-one nowadays would use "talking points" and "features" as synonyms. *Talking points* primarily refers to a featurised news story, usually long on human interest, often about a particular individual, of no great news consequence but the sort of material that gets people talking.

This leads to our first tip of tips:

Tip of tips 1: it's always the news, stupid! Given that journalism is always about news, it's crucial to be clear what news is. Many people quote the dictum, "Dog bites man isn't news; man bites dog is." The surprising or unusual is certainly one of the strongest sorts of news, but it isn't the whole of the news. There may be information that we expected (yet another price rise) but still want to hear about. It may be a story that neither concerns us directly nor particularly surprises us (an earthquake in Asia) but still engages us as citizens of the world. It may be a human interest story, referred to in the previous section, that simply intrigues us.

What these items have in common is that in some shape or form they *interest* us. So the first test for news value is that if the information won't interest readers of our target publication, it isn't news (for them).

When I lived in the United States – the home of many small-town newspapers – I worked with a man who was fond of saying: "That town's so small folks read the newspaper to see if the editor got it right." Charlie Mulcahy was joking, but he was pointing to the second test for news value: if the readers *already know it* it isn't news.

It's too easy as writers to confuse the *importance* of an issue, which may be high, with its *news value*, which may be zero. People are a company's most important asset, as the chief executive is saying *yet again*. Important? Yes. News? No.

We save ourselves wasted effort if we can spot the difference between importance and news value.

News therefore is a double-headed creature. It's information that readers don't know and which will interest them.

Tip of tips 2: stay curious, stay eager. Curiosity was suggested in Chapter 2 as the great driver of journalism. More than writing skill, stamina, unflappability, ambition and intellectual resources, it's what makes the successful freelance journalist.

We also need to be eager; otherwise curiosity withers on the vine. In other words, there are stories or situations we are curious about but can't be bothered to bring ashore.

It's natural over a long freelancing career to experience peaks and troughs of enthusiam. Nevertheless, it's a danger sign when the phone rings and we think, "Darn it, that's another commission being offered!" Burn-out is a hazard of journalism, particularly in freelancing with its loneliness and insecure income.

The second tip of tips is to cultivate the qualities of curiosity and eagerness. With them, we can look forward to a successful career in freelancing for as long as we want it.

One of the early points of this book was that freelance journalism is good for the short haul and the long haul (as well as for full-time work and part-time work). The time may come when we decide to take up other activities. The supreme appeal of freelancing is that that time may be three months, three years, 30 years – or never.

INDEX

*Freelance/freelancing, editor, commissioning editor, features, news,
newspapers and magazines all appear extensively throughout the book,
and are not indexed*

You can order these books from bookshops or direct from www.pulfordmedia.co.uk/ituri

AIR MADNESS Road's mistakes repeated
Cedric Pulford
2008 • paperback • 212 pages • £10.99 • ISBN 9780953643080
Climate, noise, safety – the shocking price of cheap flights

CASUALTY OF EMPIRE
Cedric Pulford
Britain's unpaid debt to an African kingdom
2007 • paperback • 146 pages • £11.99 • ISBN 9780953643073
Resistance and retribution at the birth of Uganda

EATING UGANDA From Christianity to Conquest
Cedric Pulford
1999 • paperback • 216 pages • £9.99 • ISBN 9780953643004

The mixed consequences of Britain's empire-building in Uganda, one of Africa's most advanced kingdoms, are explored

THE *ADVENTURES* OF SIR SAMUEL TUKE
Paul M S Hopkins
2003 • paperback • 148 pages • £9.99 • ISBN 9780953643042
Paul Hopkins supplies an authoritative introduction to this acting edition of Restoration theatre's first smash hit, *The Adventures of Five Hours* by Samuel Tuke

IMPERIAL ECHOES
Arthur Staniforth
The Sudan – People, History and Agriculture
2000 • paperback • 160 pages • £14.95 • ISBN 9781872142609
From tea with the Mahdi to soup and custard in a mud hut – a vivid picture of what empire really could be like

JOURNEY THROUGH A VANISHED WORLD
Robert Steel
Sierra Leone 1938
Edited by Colin Johnson
2001 • soft cover spiral-bound • 93 pages • £16.00 • ISBN 9780953643028
A perceptive memoir of empire, including one of the last old-style safaris before the Land Rover took over